CLOUD REVISION NOTES FOR ARTHUR CONAN DOYLE'S *THE SIGN OF FOUR* - Study guide (with AQA-style sample assessment questions and notes)

by Joe Broadfoot

All rights reserved

Copyright © Joe Broadfoot, 2017

The right of Joe Broadfoot to be identified as the author of this work has been asserted in accordance with Section 77 of the Copyright, Designs and Patents Act 1988

ISBN-13: 978-1548338053

ISBN-10: 1548338052

CLOUD 9 – 'THE SIGN OF FOUR' STUDY GUIDE

CONTENTS

INTRODUCTION: PAGE 3

CHAPTER 1: PAGE 10

CHAPTER 2: PAGE 12

CHAPTER 3: PAGE 15

CHAPTER 4: PAGE 17

CHAPTER 5: PAGE 20

CHAPTER 6: PAGE 23

CHAPTER 7: PAGE 26

CHAPTER 8: PAGE 29

CHAPTER 9: PAGE 31

CHAPTER 10: PAGE 34

CHAPTER 11: PAGE 37

CHAPTER 12: PAGE 38

AQA-STYLE ASSESSMENT MATERIAL & NOTES: PAGE 44

ESSAY-WRITING TIPS: PAGE 73

GLOSSARY: PAGE 78

Brief Introduction

This book is aimed at GCSE students of English Literature who are studying Arthur Conan Doyle's *The Sign of Four*. The focus is on what examiners are looking for, especially since the changes to the curriculum in 2015, and here you will find each chapter covered in detail. We hope this will help you and be a valuable tool in your studies and revision.

Criteria for high marks

Make sure you use appropriate critical language (see glossary of literary terms at the back). You need your argument to be fluent, well-structured and coherent. Stay focused!

Analyse and explore the use of form, structure and the language. Explore how these aspects affect the meaning.

Make connections between texts and look at different interpretations. Explore their strengths and weaknesses. Don't forget to use supporting references to strengthen your argument.

Analyse and explore the context.

.

Other tips

Make your studies active!

Don't just sit there reading! Never forget to annotate, annotate and annotate!

All page references refer to the 2014 reprinted paperback edition of *The Sign of Four* published by Penguin English Library, London (ISBN: 978-0-141-39548-7).

The Sign of Four

AQA (New specification starting in 2015)

If you're studying for an AQA qualification in English Literature, there's a good chance your teachers will choose this text to study. There are good reasons for that: it's moralistic in that the text encourages us to think about right and wrong.

The Sign of Four is one of the texts listed on Paper 1, which needs to be completed in 1 hours 45 minutes. As well as knowing a nineteenth-century text from back-to-front, students will also be expected to know a Shakespearean play in full. More about that later.

Bear in mind, that you also need to be prepared for Paper 2, which consists of answering essay questions on a modern text, and on two poems categorised as 'Unseen Poetry' and two poems from the AQA anthology.

AQA have given students a choice of 12 set texts for the Modern Texts section of the exam paper. There are 6 plays: JB Priestley's *An Inspector Calls*, Willy Russell's *Blood Brothers*, Alan Bennett's *The History Boys*, Dennis Kelly's *DNA*, Simon Stephens's script of *The Curious Incident of the Dog* in the *Night-Time*, and Shelagh Delaney's *A Taste of Honey*. Alternatively, students can chose to write on the following 6 novels: William Golding's *Lord of the Flies*, AQA's Anthology called *Telling Tales*, George Orwell's *Animal Farm*, Kazuo Ishiguro's *Never Let Me Go*, Meera Syal's *Anita and Me*, and Stephen Kelman's *Pigeon English*. Answering one essay question on one of the above is worth a total of 34 marks, which includes 4 for vocabulary, spelling, punctuation and grammar. In other words, this section is worth 21.25% of your total grade at GCSE.

AQA have produced a poetry anthology entitled *Poems, Past and Present*, which includes 30 poems. Rather than study all 30, students are to study one of the two clusters of 15, which concentrate on common themes. There are two themes which students can choose from: Love and relationships, or power and conflict. Within the chosen thematic cluster, students must study all 15 poems and be prepared to write on any of them. Answering this section is worth 18.75% of your total GCSE grade.

The 'unseen poetry' section is more demanding, in that students will not know what to expect. However, as long as they are prepared to comment and compare different poems in terms of their content, theme, structure and language, students should be ready for whatever the exam can throw at them. This section is worth 20% of your total grade at GCSE.

CLOUD 9 – 'THE SIGN OF FOUR' STUDY GUIDE

Paper 2 itself makes up 60% of your total grade or, in other words, 96 raw marks. Just under half of those marks, 44 to be exact (27.5% of 60%), can be gained from analysing how the writer uses language, form and structure to create effects. To get a high grade, it is necessary for students to use appropriate literary terms, like metaphors, similes and so on.

AO1 accounts for 36 marks of the total of 96 (22.5% of the 60% for Paper 2, to be exact). To score highly on AO1, students need to provide an informed personal response, using quotations to support their point of view.

AO3 is all about context and, like Paper 1, only 7.5% of the total mark is awarded for this knowledge (12 marks). Similarly, AO4 (which is about spelling, punctuation and grammar) only accounts for 2.5% of the total (4 marks).

Now let's go back to Paper 1. One of the difficulties with Paper 1 is the language. That can't be helped, bearing in mind that part A of the exam paper involves answering questions on Shakespeare, whereas part B is all about the 19th-century novel.

To further complicate things, the education system is in a state of flux: that means we have to be ready for constant change. Of course, everyone had got used to grades A,B and C meaning a pass. It was simple, it was straightforward and nearly everyone understood it. Please be prepared that from this day henceforward, the top grade will now be known as 9. A grade 4 will be a pass, and anything below that will be found and anything above it will be a pass. Hopefully, that's not too confusing for anyone!

Now onto the exam itself. As I said, Paper 1 consists of Shakespeare and the 19th-century novel. Like Paper 2, it is a written closed book exam (in other words you are not allowed to have the texts with you), which lasts one hour 45 minutes. You can score 64 marks, which amounts to 40% of your GCSE grade.

In section B, students will be expected to write in detail about an extract from the novel they have studied in class and then write about the novel as a whole. Just for the record, the choices of novel are the following: *The Strange Case of Dr Jekyll and Mr Hyde* by Robert Louis Stevenson, *A Christmas Carol* and *Great Expectations* by Charles Dickens, *Jane Eyre* by Charlotte Brontë, *Frankenstein* by Mary Shelley, *Pride and Prejudice* by Jane Austin, and *The Sign of Four* by Sir Arthur Conan Doyle.

Another important thing to consider is the fact that for section B of Paper 1, you will not be assessed on Assessment Objective 4 (AO4), which involves spelling, punctuation, grammar and vocabulary. This will be assessed on section A of Paper 1, which is about Shakespeare, and it will be worth 2.5% of your overall GCSE grade. In terms of raw marks, it is worth 4 out of 64. So for once, we need not concern ourselves with what is affectionately known as 'SPAG' too much on this part of Paper 1.

CLOUD 9 – 'THE SIGN OF FOUR' STUDY GUIDE

However, it is necessary to use the correct literary terminology wherever possible to make sure we maximise our marks on Assessment Objective2 (AO2). AO2 tests how well we can analyse language form and structure. Additionally, we are expected to state the effect the writer tried to create and how it impacts on the reader.

This brings me onto Assessment Objective 1 (AO1), which involves you writing a personal response to the text. It is important that you use quotations to backup your points of view. Like AO2, AO1 is worth 15% of your GCSE on Paper 1.

Assessment Objective 3 (AO3) is worth half of that, but nevertheless it is important to comment on context to make sure you get as much of the 7.5% up for grabs as you can.

So just to make myself clear, there are 30 marks available in section B for your answer on the 19th-century novel. Breaking it down even further, you will get 12 marks maximum the backing up your personal opinion with quotations, an additional 12 marks for analysing the writer's choice of words for effect (not forgetting to use appropriate terminology - more on that see the glossary at the back of this book), and six marks for discussing context.

As you can see, we've got a lot to get through so without further ado let's get on with the actual text itself and possible exam questions.

Previous exam questions

Notwithstanding the governmental changes to the grading system, it is still good practice to go over previous exam papers. To make sure that you meet AQA's learning objectives and get a high mark, make sure you go into the exam knowing something about the following:

- the plot

- the characters

- the theme

- selected quotations/details

- exam skills

Page-by-page analysis

Chapter One

The opening chapter is entitled 'The Science of Deduction', so clearly the focus is going to be on private investigator Sherlock Holmes's method of detection (1). We may feel surprised that he can detect anything, given that he is 'scarred with innumerable puncture-marks', which suggests he's an inveterate drug-user (1).

His 'companion', Dr Watson, who also narrates, takes Holmes to task for his bad habit. We discover that Watson is afraid of confronting Holmes, but does it anyway. However, the doctor needs 'Beaune' wine to fuel his courage, which suggests that he is a meek character generally (1).

Watson is also physically weak commodes to Holmes, as 'the Afghan campaign' of 1878-80 has taken its toll on him (2). Consequently, he cannot 'throw any extra strain upon' his 'constitution' (2).

We also discover that Watson is quite sentimental, at least in comparison to Holmes, who complains that his 'brochure' entitled 'A Study in Scarlet' is tinged 'with romanticism' (3). Holmes believes that the account should have been more about his 'unravelling' of 'curious analytical reasoning from effects to causes' (3). This suggests a huge ego and an obsession with science.

Holmes is very much a specialist and admits he has 'been guilty of several monographs', which indicate that he has been keeping busy writing in detail on subjects, such as: 'Upon the distinction between the Ashes of the Various Tobaccos' (4). Watson acknowledges his companion's 'genius for minutiae', which is an appropriate skill for a detective (5).

When he guesses that Watson has been to the post office, we discover how Holmes operates as a detective. Holmes reveals that if you 'eliminate all other factors' then 'the one that remains must be the truth' (6).

Nevertheless, Watson thinks he has stumped the detective, when he gives a watch as a test to see if Holmes can uncover anything about 'the character or habits of the late owner' (6). Much to Watson's chagrin, Holmes reveals that the previous owner was 'a man of untidy habits', who final took 'to drink' (7). Watson is upset because the previous owner was his late brother. For all his brilliance, Holmes realises he has been callous, saying: 'I had forgotten how personal and painful a thing it might be to you'

(7). Although Holmes is a genius, he seems to struggle when it comes to conducting himself in a social situation.

This time, Holmes has worked out the truth through the application of 'the balance of probability' (8). There follows a detailed explanation of how he has put together a whole story through scraps of evidence.

However, he needs a greater challenge than the tests provided by Watson to keep him away from drugs. His stagnation is represented through the pathetic fallacy of 'the yellow fog' (9). The 'dun-coloured houses' show how bored he feels by his current jobless predicament (9).

Luckily, an adventure seems set to begin as his landlady, Mrs Hudson announces the arrival of 'Miss Mary Morstan' (9). The reader wonders what this alliteratively-named probable femme fatale could possibly want with Sherlock Holmes.

Chapter Two

In the second chapter, entitled 'The Statement of the Case', we quickly discover that Miss Morstan is quite exotic: her 'turban' suggests that she has some connection with India. The narrator thinks she may be far from well off, as the 'simplicity about her costume' suggests 'limited means' (10).

While she oozes vulnerability and 'intense inward agitation' with her trembling lip and quivering hand, Holmes is the opposite. The contrast is emphasised by the description of 'his clear-cut, hawk-like features' (11). This shows he is like a predator, while she is prey in comparison.

We find out that the date is some time in late 1888 and that her father 'was an officer in an Indian regiment', which explains the turban (11). Her 'unfortunate father' has gone missing and she needs Holmes to investigate his inexplicable disappearance (11).

There are no obvious clues in his luggage, and the only friend he has in England is 'Major Sholto' (12). To add to the mystery, Miss Morstan tells Holmes that she has received a 'very large lustrous pearl' every year since, on the advice of her employer, she published her address in answer to an advertisement (12).

She also shows Holmes a letter which, amongst other things, tells her that she is 'a wronged woman' who 'shall have justice' (13). She is told to meet the letter-writer outside the Lyceum Theatre, but warned not to 'bring police' (13).

However, she can 'bring two friends' (13). Luckily, Holmes and Watson are willing to take on the case and accompany her.

Although fascinated by the idea of solving the case, Holmes's lack of interest in people is evidenced by his comment that he 'did not observe' that Miss Morstan is 'attractive' (14). Watson is flabbergasted and calls Holmes 'an automaton - a calculating machine' (14). Once again, we see reason represented by Holmes opposed to Watson's 'emotional qualities' (14).

Holmes recommends that Watson read Winewood Reade's 'Martyrdom of Man', while he disappears for an hour (15). The intertextual reference suggests that Holmes is a social Darwinist, who believes in survival of the fittest rather than religion and sentimentality.

Watson, meanwhile, remains preoccupied with the 27-year-old Miss Morstan, who he describes as at a 'sweet age' (15). He recognizes that ideas of a romance with her are 'mere will-o'-the-whisps of the imagination' (15). He describes his future as 'black', which shows a deep pessimism on his part.

Chapter Three

The third chapter entitled 'In Quest of a Solution' begins at 5:30, when Holmes returns. He seems to think it's an open and shut case, saying: 'there is no great mystery in this matter (16). Sometimes, the renowned detective suffers from over-confidence, and this is an example of it.

The narrative uses Watson's obtuseness or comparatively slow understanding to tease out more information from Holmes in a form that is digestible for the reader. Holmes explains that he thinks 'Sholto's heir knows something [...] and desires to make compensation' (16). Watson is an excellent foil for Holmes, as he questions his companion by saying: 'It is too much to suppose that her father is still alive' (17).

The tension increases as Holmes takes 'his revolver from his drawer' (17). This suggests that he is taking the matter seriously with the expectation of violence. Miss Morstan 'pale' face adds to the impression that something dramatic is about to happen (17).

She shows Holmes a paper that was found in her father's desk, which reads: 'The sign of the four - Jonathan Small, Mahomet Singh,

Abdullah Khan, Dost Akbar' (18). Holmes has to admit that he does 'not see how' it 'bears upon the matter', but nevertheless tells her to 'preserve it carefully' (18). Even if the characters do not know it, the reader is aware that it will be an important document as it echoes the title of the novel. The 'fog' that envelopes them emphasises the lack of clarity surrounding the case (18).

At the meeting place, 'a small, dark, brisk man in the dress of a coachman' accosts them, checking that the police are not with them (19). He whistles to a ragged street urchin (known as street Arabs at that time), who takes them to a four-wheel vehicle. Then they are whisked away. It is all so mysterious, as the utmost secrecy appears to be expected.

It appears that Watson has maintained his relationship with Miss Marston, as he remarks that: 'To this day she declares that I told her one moving anecdote as to how a musket looked into my tent' (20). He is relating his scary 'adventures in Afghanistan', but the 'broad, silent water' of the Thames, which they cross seems just as threatening (20).

They eventually reach 'a questionable and forbidding neighbourhood' in south London (20). Even the brick buildings are 'staring' (20). 'A

Hindoo servant, clad in a yellow turban' opens the door (20). A 'high, piping voice from some inner room' is heard beckoning them in (20). The chapter ends on this cliffhanger as the reader wonders who the voice belongs to.

Chapter Four

There is a certain amount of horror in the scene that follows, as 'a blaze of yellow light' streams out, reminiscent of some similarly-colored scenes from Frankenstein (22).

Their host is 'a small man with 'a bald shining scalp which' shoots out of his 'bristle of red hair' 'like a mountain-peak from fir-trees' (22). His description relates directly to the title of the chapter: 'The Story of the Bald-headed Man' (22). We quickly get the idea that the host is mentally unstable as 'his features' are 'in a perpetual jerk' (22).

The 30-year-old describes his home as 'an oasis of art in the howling desert of South London' (22). By saying this, he displays considerable vanity. The reader must feel his portrayal is extremely unsympathetic.

He introduces himself as 'Thaddeus Sholto' and asks Doctor Watson to check his 'mitral valve' (23). Watson can only gauge that Thaddeus is 'in an ecstasy of fear', which is almost an oxymoron (23). The impression is that Thaddeus virtually enjoys being afraid, as if he has masochist tendencies.

Thaddeus makes his brother sound like an intimidating person and he warns the group that 'nothing would annoy Brother Bartholomew more than any publicity' (23).

When Thaddeus blinks his 'weak, watery blue eyes' it reminds us of his lack of physical strength (24) However, the reader may distrust Thaddeus professed 'shrinking from all forms of rough materialism', given that he is surrounded by opulence and riches (24).

Watson suggests that they should set off immediately to Norwood to 'see Brother Bartholomew' given the later hour, but Thaddeus laughs 'until his ears' are 'quite red' (25). This shows that Thaddeus is quite contemptuous of other as he seems to look down condescendingly on Watson's quite sensible suggestion.

Thaddeus relates the story of his father, who admitted on his death bed that he had been afflicted by a 'cursed greed' that prevented him from sharing 'the treasure' with Miss Morstan.

The reader may imagine that, like his father, Thaddeus may be guilty of 'avarice' (26).

Thaddeus's father claimed on his death bed that Captain Morstan had always had 'a weak heart', which makes the reader think there may be a family connection to Thaddeus and his 'mitral valve' (27, 23). It is claimed that the Captain 'sprung out of his chair' as they argued over 'the treasure' and fell cutting his head (27). Thaddeus's father kept the subsequent death secret for fear of being accused of murder.

Just when Thaddeus's father was about to tell his sons where the treasure was hidden, 'a bearded, hairy face, with cruel eyes' was seen peering through the window (28). Initially, the only evidence the twins can find is 'a single foot-mark' in 'the flower bed' (28). Later, 'a torn piece of paper with the words "The sign of the four" scrawled across it' was found' (28, 29).

Like a stereotypical Victorian female, Miss Morstan is 'about to faint', after hearing this account (29). By contrast, the heroic Holmes is leaning back 'with an abstracted expression' (29). Holmes is clearly fascinated by the case, as his eyes are described as 'glittering' (29).

Thaddeus, meanwhile, speaks in French, which translated means: 'Bad taste leads to crime'

(30). It reminds the reader that his 'oasis' may be considered by some to be in bad taste. Perhaps this is a clue leading us to the real criminal, which we may suspect is Thaddeus.

As they prepare to go out, 'no part of' Thaddeus is 'visible save his mobile and peaky face' (31). This indicates that metaphorically he may be hiding the truth. There is nothing honest nor wholesome about his presentation. The idea that he is a 'hyperchondriac' is repeated throughout the chapter, making the reader distrust him (32).

Thaddeus has taken over the narrative for much of this chapter, and this is further embedded by the use of his father as narrator. As in 'Frankenstein', the writer uses embedded narratives to add tension and mystery to the plot.

Chapter Five

The chapter is entitled: 'The Tragedy of Pondicherry Lodge' and, by 11pm, they reach the place mentioned (33). The title warns us to expect something awful and this is further foreshadowed by 'half a moon peeping' through 'heavy clouds' (33). This seems the perfect setting for some unspeakable gothic crime.

The building is 'vast' and, with 'its gloom and its deadly silence', it strikes 'a chill to the heart' (34). Bartholomew's window is 'where the moonlight strikes', highlighting a possible place where something heinous has been committed (34). Using the sound imagery of the housekeeper, Mrs Bernstein, 'whimpering', the narrator conveys to the that something awful has indeed happened (34).

Meanwhile, the horror of the situation draws Miss Morstan closer to Watson, as he discovers 'her hand' in his (34). He thinks it is 'instinct' that has made her 'turn' to him 'for comfort' (35). Unlike Holmes, he is forever looking for emotional explanations for behaviour.

Holmes remains in control of the situation and never lets his emotions get the better of him. While Thaddeus's teeth are 'chattering', Holmes is looking for evidence with 'his lens' (37). Watson assists Thaddeus, whose knees are 'trembling', but Holmes is only focused on solving the case (37).

'Moonlight' illuminates the death scene, as we see the grisly smiling face of a recently deceased Batholomew through the keyhole (38). This method of viewing the scene makes it all the more mysterious, as Holmes and Watson can only see part of the room until they break the door down.

Once inside, they can see 'a peculiar instrument - a brown, close-grained stick, with a stone head like a hammer, rudely lashed on with coarse twine' (39). At this stage, it is difficult to imagine exactly how this implement was used in the murder, but the reader trusts that Holmes will work out how it fits into the crime scene. Unsurprisingly, a note with 'the sign of the four' written on it is read there. Less predictably, the dead man has 'what looked like a long dark thorn stuck in his skin just above the war' (39). Holmes informs Watson that the thorn is 'poisoned' (39).

Then Thaddeus's cries out that: 'The treasure is gone!' (39). He claims he left Bartholomew at 'ten o'clock' and that now the police will blame him for the murder as he was the last one to see him (40). Strangely, Holmes reassures Thaddeus, telling him: 'You have no reason for fear, Mr Sholto' (40). This is uncharacteristic of Holmes, as earlier in the novel he tells Watson that 'a client is a [...] mere unit, a factor in a problem' (40). Suddenly, he seems less like the automaton that Watson accused him of being, and more like a human being.

Chapter Six

We learn a little more about Holmes's character at the beginning of this chapter, entitled 'Sherlock Holmes Gives a Demonstration' (41). He displays a superior attitude when telling Watson to 'just sit in the corner' (41). While he clearly values Watson's companionship, he doesn't treat him like an equal.

The narrative switches to the present tense, adding tension, as Holmes explains that the 'wooden-legged' suspect was aided by an 'ally' (42). He tells Watson that 'this ally breaks fresh ground in the annals of crime in this country' (42). By contrast, Holmes uses the past tense to describe the one-legged suspect, which makes him sound less dangerous as the threat is less immediate.

He continues to talk to Watson, as a teacher would to a pupil, saying: 'How often have I said to you that when you have eliminated the impossible, whatever remains, however improbable, must be the truth?' (43). Through the use of this rhetorical question, Holmes mildly scolds Watson.

The narrator compares Holmes to a bird, with his 'long thin nose' and his 'beady eyes gleaming' (44). Perhaps it refers to the detective's ability to pick the wheat from the chaff: an essential gift when choosing which clues to follow-up. Holmes has to be careful not to spend time on red herrings, or irrelevant clues.

Watson is useful to him, though, to confirm what he believes. Holmes uses him as a sounding board. For instance, when he asks his 'conclusion' as to the cause of Bartholomew's death (45). Watson replies that it was caused by 'some vegetable alkaloid' (45). He adds it was from 'some strychnine-like substance which would produce tetanus' (45). Holmes said that occurred to him 'the instant' he 'saw the drawn muscles of the face' (45). Once again, Holmes retains the upper hand in his dealings with his companion.

The next character we are introduced to is a police detective called Athelney Jones. He is described as a 'very stout, portly man in a grey suit' and seems to be the opposite of Holmes (46). Jones repeats himself, by saying: 'Here's a business' and then by saying: 'Here's a pretty business' (46). His method of detection is 'common sense', so he is worlds apart from Holmes, who is much more scientific in his approach (46).

Holmes is clearly more sophisticated than the 'fat detective' as, like Thaddeus, he can speak French (47). The translation of Holmes's French phrase is: 'There are no fools so troublesome as those that have some wit'. Holmes is quoting Francois de la Rochefoucauld, a French nobleman, with whom he shares the view that human conduct should neither be condemned nor celebrated. However, Holmes is observing that Jones is an idiot, who is not completely devoid of intelligence and that makes him a nuisance at times.

Jones refers to Holmes dismissively as 'Mr Theorist', when the latter reassures Thaddeus that he will be able to 'clear' him 'of the charge' of murder (48). It is obvious from this comment that Jones thinks of himself as more practical than Holmes. Nevertheless, Holmes tells Jones the identity of one of the suspected one-legged man: 'Jonathan Small' (48).

Holmes has no confidence in Jones's ability to find the real murderer, as he suggests leaving him 'to exult over any mare's nest which he may choose to construct' (49). The 'mare's nest' expression refers to someone's ability to discover something seemingly amazing, which doesn't actually exist. However, Holmes does believe in old Sherman's dog, Toby, so sends

Watson off to bring back the 'queer mongrel' (49).

Before Watson heads off, Holmes quotes the 'pithy' German philosopher Goethe. The translation is: 'We are used to seeing that Man despises what he never comprehends' (50). It clearly refers to Jones, wrongly accusing Thaddeus, perhaps because of his exotic appearance which defies understanding.

Chapter Seven

This chapter is entitled: 'The Episode of the Barrel', so we can expect this object to be instrumental, at least in this part of the story (51).

However, it begins with Watson revealing his reluctance to take advantage of Miss Morstan's 'weeping' (51). He says it was 'the effort of self-restraint' which held him back. He seems a perfect gentleman, an excellent foil for a stereotypical Victorian woman.

When he leaves Miss Morstan with her employer, Mrs Cecil Forrester, he describes the pair as 'two graceful, clinging figures' illuminated by 'the hall-light shining through stained glass' (52). It shows the pair in a holy light suggesting purity.

Then we meet Mr Sherman, who is described as 'a lanky, lean old man with stooping shoulders, a stringy neck, and blue-tinted glasses' (53). Reading between the lines we can guess that he is hard-working, which has the 'stooping shoulders', but mildly eccentric, judging by the blue lenses.

Holmes, meanwhile, makes it clear that he is on Thaddeus's side, as he calls him 'friend' (54). He is clearly disgusted with Jones's arrests of Thaddeus, 'the gatekeeper, the housekeeper, and the Indian servant' (54). Taking the police sergeant's 'bull's eye', or small lantern, Holmes tries to get to the bottom of the mystery (54).

He asks Watson to 'loose the dog, and look out for Blondin', referring to the nineteenth-century escapologist, who was a famous tightrope walker (55). Adding to Holmes's magical aura is Watson comment that he's 'like an enormous glow-worm (55).

The dog is also revered for his ability to sniff out a criminal. Watson says that he's 'like a connoisseur sniffling the bouquet of a famous vintage' (56).

The setting the dog leads them to is incredibly depressing, 'with its scattered dirt-heaps and ill-grown shrubs', which have 'a blighted, ill-omened look' (57). All is decay, which is a common theme of turn of the century literature.

Holmes reveals that 'Jonathan Small did not get the treasure because he and his associates were themselves convicts' (58). He explains that Major Sholto was 'happy in the possession of the treasure' until he received a letter 'to say that the men whom he had wronged' were no longer in prison (58). Holmes arrogantly says that 'it is the only hypothesis which covers all the facts' (58).

He goes on to explain how Small wanted to regain 'his rights' to the treasure and get 'revenge on the man who had wronged him' (59). He left the 'sign' to show the act of murder was 'something in the nature of an act of justice' (59).

He believes that Small was aided by the 'butler, Lal Rao' (59). He adds that Mrs Bernsteing gives Rao 'far from a good character' (59). This seems strangely unscientific of Holmes, who is not usually prone to jumping to conclusions.

Indeed, he is more of a philosopher, proved when he asks Watson if he is 'well up' in his studies of 'Jean Paul' Richter (60). Holmes goes on to cite Richter's idea that 'the chief proof of man's real greatness lies in his perception of his own smallness' (61). This suggests that egotism has no place for the truly great people of this world, but in Holmes's case concerns his considerable eye for detail.

Eventually, Toby the dog leads them to a 'barrel', which causes the narrator and Holmes to 'burst simultaneously into an uncontrollable fit of laughter' (62). On the surface, it seems that the intervention of the dog has yielded no results, at this stage. The reader wonder what exactly this means, so the chapter is ended on a cliffhanger of sorts.

Chapter Eight

It is almost as if the dog is Holmes's gothic double, as Watson notes: 'Toby has lost his character for infallibility' (63). By trusting the dog's instincts, Holmes has taken Watson on a wild goose chase. However, Holmes will not give up.

He has a huge ego, which means he underestimates others. This is proven when he says: 'These fellows are sharper than I expected' (64).

As the pair follow the dog chasing a different scent trail to the river, they encounter Mrs Smith and her son, Jack. From her, they discover that the 'wooden-legged man' is a 'monkey-faced chap' with a 'voice, which is kind o' thick and foggy' (65). This description associates this criminal with mysterious weather, where nothing is clear.

Holmes explains that to get information from 'people of that sort' you must 'never let them' know that what they've said is valuable to you, or they 'will instantly shut up like an oyster' (66). This simile conveys the idea that the Smiths are a seafaring family. Additionally, we become aware of Holmes condescending attitude to the lower classes, when he says 'people of that sort'.

He displays the same attitude in his dealings with 'The Baker Street Irregulars', who the chapter is named after. He describes Wiggins, the leader of the group as his 'dirty little lieutenant' (67).

Meanwhile, Watson explains his dilemma. Being a moral man, he chooses to follow the righteous path of trying to deliver 'the treasure' to Miss Morstan, although he admits that if he finds it, it will 'probably put her forever beyond' his reach (68). He believes that as a rich heiress, she will be inundated with suitors and he will have no chance of winning her love.

We then meet 'the ragged little street Arabs', who are the aforementioned 'unofficial' child police force of Baker Street 'irregulars'. Wiggins is described as 'a disreputable little scarecrow' by the narrator. This makes it clear that Watson has little regard for Holmes's young allies.

After the irregulars are sent on their mission to 'find the whereabouts of a steam launch called "Aurora"', Holmes begins explaining who is responsible for the 'diminutive foot-marks' at the scene of the crime (70, 71). He says that a 'savage' from the 'Andaman Islands' must have fired the dart from 'a blow pipe' into Bartholomew's neck (71). The word 'savage' is offensive to modern readers, due to the inherent racism implied. However, during Victorian times, many readers would have not thought the term to be derisory.

Holmes reads to Watson from his latest 'gazetteer', which shows he is quite erudite and well-informed for his time (71). He quotes the book to inform Watson that: 'The aborigines of the Andaman Islands may perhaps claim the distinction of being the smallest race upon this earth' (72).

After all this mental work, Holmes takes 'up his violin' (72). This proves he is a genius in more than one field, as in music also he shows 'a remarkable gift for improvisation' (73).

Chapter Nine

We see Holmes's commitment to a lifelong education again, as he is 'deep in a book', when Watson awakes at the start of the chapter entitled: 'A Break in the Chain' (74).

CLOUD 9 – 'THE SIGN OF FOUR' STUDY GUIDE

Watson is shocked by Holmes's sexist misogyny, as he warns his friend that 'women are never to be entirely trusted' (74). Watson calls it an 'atrocious sentiment', emphasizes their difference of opinion on the fairer sex.

Although he is instructed not to reveal too much to Miss Morstan and Mrs Forrester, the latter's comment that the story of Bartholomew's death is 'a romance' suggests he may have given them quite a detailed account (75). Both ladies know that the story includes 'an injured lady, half a million in treasure, a black cannibal, and a wooden-legged ruffian' (75).

Miss Mary Morstan shows 'no sign of elation at the prospect' of becoming rich (75). This shows how virtuous she is, as Watson notes.

Meanwhile, Holmes shows an obsessive side to his character, as he is portrayed walking up and down rather than sleeping at night. As he readily admits, the 'infernal problem is consuming' him (76).

Possibly to take his mind off the case, Holmes busies himself with what Watson calls a 'malodorous chemical experiment' (77). The reader may suspect that this activity has something to do with solving the case.

Later, Holmes changes into 'a rude sailor dress' to go 'down the river' (77). He instructs Watson to 'remain' as his 'representative', as he expects news at any moment (77).

It is clear that Holmes trusts Watson, as he also instructs him 'to act on' his 'own judgement if any news should come' (78). However, nothing initially materialises except a report in the newspaper, revealing that Thaddeus and the housekeeper have been released without charge by the police.

Watson also notes how 'ingenious' Holmes is to put an advertisement in the same paper, asking for information about 'the whereabouts of [...] Mordecai Smith and the launch "Aurora"' (79). By saying that the information is being requested by Mrs Smith, Watson believes that Holmes is disguising the fact that it is he who actual seeks her husband and the boat. However, perhaps some criminals may recognise Holmes's address: '221B, Baker Street, which is also in the advertisement.

A 'downcast' Jones arrives at Baker Street, looking for Holmes, whom he describes as 'a wonderful man' (80). However, the policemen takes 'satisfaction' from the fact that Holmes 'has been at fault too' (81). This suggests a deep rivalry between the two men.

When Holmes turns up in disguise, both Jones and Watson are fooled by his 'aged' appearance, until his normal 'voice' breaks in 'upon' them (81, 82). Jones commends Holmes's impression of a 'workhouse cough', alluding to the miserable conditions endured by the poverty-stricken during the Victorian era (83).

It seems that Holmes is a man of many talents, as he vows to impress Jones and Watson with his 'merits as a housekeeper' (84). This suggests Holmes's extreme versatility and confidence.

Chapter Ten

We find out in alliterative terms that the trio's 'meal' is a 'merry one' (85). The repeating 'm' sound suggests music and enjoyment, a radical departure from Holmes's 'black depression' earlier (85).

Holmes reveals that he did indeed plunge himself into 'a chemical analysis' to take his mind off the case (86). This enabled him to consider Small's 'delicate finesse', which he claims 'is usually a product of higher education' (86). His admiration for Small's 'cunning' is clearly growing (86).

Holmes explains that Small would be unlikely to set off immediately in the 'Aurora', as his 'lair would be too valuable' to give up 'until he was sure that he could do without it' (87). The name of the boat foreshadows the idea that there might be a lot of light illuminating the darkness later, like the Northern Lights that it is named after.

While he was in disguise, Holmes reveals that he encountered the boat's owner, Mordecai Smith. Holmes seems to have little regard for him as he describes him as 'the worse for liquor' (88). The detective clearly thinks that Mordecai is like other men of his class, prone to 'chucking shillings about' when he feels 'flush of money' (88). This working class man is being portrayed as a foolish character, who spends his ill-gotten gains on alcohol.

We get the idea that Holmes is a gambler, from his comment that 'it is a hundred to one' that Smith knows where Small and the Islander are (89). Holmes is quite exact with his odds, as he claims that it is 'ten to one that they go downstream' (89). From this we get the impression that Holmes is very calculating and mathematical in his approach to solving mysteries.

This is further emphasised by his insistence that 'you can say with precision what an average number [of people] will be up to', although he admits that 'individuals vary' (90). He has taken on the above theory from his study of Winwood Reade, an author he recommended to Watson earlier.

As the trio and their helpers start their pursuit of the 'Aurora', the pace of the narrative picks up, with the characters beginning to use shorter sentences mixed with imperatives like: 'Full speed ahead, engineer' (90).

Before long 'the dull blur in front of' them turns into 'the dainty "Aurora"' (91). This shows literally how the mystery is slowly unravelling as the criminals come into view.

CLOUD 9 – 'THE SIGN OF FOUR' STUDY GUIDE

The Islander is unflatteringly described as 'a little black man [...] with a great, misshapen head and a shock of tangled, dishevelled hair' (92). The term 'unhallowed dwarf' makes the Islander appear diabolical, while his 'strong yellow teeth gnashing' suggest he is no more than an animal (92). By dehumanizing the Islander, the writer ensures that the reader has little or no sympathy for him.

The chapter is entitled: 'The End of the Islander', so it is no real surprise when he is shot and falls 'into the stream' (93). Even then, the narrator comments on the Islander's 'venomous, menacing eyes' (94). The reader may wonder whether or not the Islander is actually dead as there is 'no sign' of him thereafter.

Meanwhile, Small gets stuck in the mud-bank and is hauled in 'like some evil fish', along with the two Smiths and the treasure (93). Like the Islander, so far Small has no redeemable characteristics.

Finally, the writer personifies 'the horrible death' that 'passed so close' to Holmes and Watson 'that night' to emphasise how they flirt with danger. Watson is the more sensitive, as the thought turns him 'sick', while Holmes smiles and shrugs 'his shoulders' (94). This proves how nonchalant Holmes is compared to his sidekick.

Chapter Eleven

In this chapter entitled: 'The Great Agra Treasure' we get the point of view of Small (95). He seems motivated by greed, judging by his 'twinkling eyes' that look 'at the box which had been the cause of his ill-doings' (95). Small admits he 'welted' the Islander 'with the slack end of the rope' for killing Bartholomew, which sounds quite barbaric (95). This was because he 'had no quarrel whatever' with 'this young Sholto' (96).

Meanwhile, Jones is a self-congratulatory mood now that Small is in handcuffs and the case seems to have been resolved. Watson notes that Jones 'was already beginning to give himself airs on the strength of the capture' (97).

When Watson goes to deliver the treasure to Miss Morstan, she appears 'dressed in some sort of white diaphanous material' (98). This makes her seem angelic.

Watson seems impetuous in her presence as he tells her that she and Thaddeus 'will have a couple of hundred thousand each' (99). She seems less than impressed though, as there is 'no eagerness in her voice' (99).

When it turns out that the box is 'empty', Watson can contain himself no longer. He explains his joy to Miss Morstan when he says: 'You are within my reach again' (100). He ends the chapter by saying that he 'gained' 'a treasure' as Mary Morstan reciprocates his love.

Chapter Twelve

Another embedded narrative is about to add a touch more realism to the novel, as the chapter title suggests we will discover 'The Strange Story of Jonathan Small' (101).

Small is still a less than sympathetic character, as he is portrayed leaning 'back in his chair' and laughing 'aloud' when Watson shows him the empty box (101). At this stage, the reader may feel that Miss Morstan has been deprived of the treasure that is rightly hers by a depraved criminal.

Apparently, according to Small, the treasure has been 'scattered' in the river (102). Once he drops 'his mask of stoicism', the reader has a chance to find out what has motivated Small to commit these criminal acts (103).

Through his embedded narrative, Small takes the reader back in time to 1857 and the start of the Indian Rebellion, which he calls 'the great mutiny' (104). He had joined the 'Third Buffs', an army regiment on active service in India (103). He calls it a time of 'perfect hell', with 'two hundred thousand black devils let loose' (104). Clearly, for today's reader this language sounds incredibly racist, but even Victorian readers would have had little sympathy for this character, albeit for different reasons.

Small seems to think that the indigenous people of India are inferior, as he describes the country as being 'up like a swarm of bees' (105). Bu comparing them to 'bees' and by using the word 'swarm', Small dehumanises the Indian rebels, making them sound like insects.

The word 'swarming' is used by Small to describe 'the city of Agra', which again suggests that the inhabitants are less than human (106). However, he clearly has a higher regard for his 'Punjabees', whom he describes as 'tall, fierce-looking chaps, Mahomet Singh and Abdullah Khan' (107).

These two 'Sikhs' attack him when he lays his 'musket down to strike a match' and hold him at knife-point and gun-point (108). They tell Small that he must chose to join them or die. Small agrees to join them as long as it is not 'against the safety of the fort' (109). Luckily for him, they want him to help them to secure some 'loot' (109). There seems to be honour amongst thieves, as they swear that the treasure must be 'equally divided among the four' of them (109). The additional person involved is 'Dost Akbar', whom Small has not yet met (109).

Singh and Khan tell Small the story of the 'rajah' and his hoarding of 'gold' (109, 110). They are unhappy with the rajah's unwillingness to take sides in the Indian Rebellion, so are resolved to rob him. The rajah has appointed his 'trusty servant', 'Achmet' to look after the rajah's treasure and to deposit it safely in the fort (110). Khan tells Small that his 'foster-brother Dost Akbar' will lead Achmet 'to a side-postern of the fort' where Singh and Khan will lie in wait (110).

Small says that Achmet's life 'was a thing as light as air' to him (110, 111). Once again, this shows him to be an unrepentant murderer. The reader is unlikely to have any sympathy with such a character.

Through pathetic fallacy, the narrative suggests the enormity of the crime about to take place. Small reveals that 'the rain was falling steadily', indicating that something awful is about to happen (111).

Small describes Achmet as 'a little fat, round fellow', who 'seemed to be all in a quiver with fear' (112). It seems even more merciless and cold-blooded to kill such a weak and helpless man. Even Small admits that 'the more' he 'looked at his fat, frightened face, the harder did it seem that we should slay him in cold blood' (113). However, the thought just makes him want 'to get it over' (113). When Achmet tries to escape, Small trips him and Akbar plunges a 'knife twice in his side' (113).

What perturbs Watson most is the 'flippant and careless way' that Small is narrating his story. The reader is reminded once again, that the crimes Small has committed are heinous (114). The moral seems to be that greed can lead to crime.

We return to Small's narrative, as he explains how they cover Achmet's body 'with loose bricks', which is anything but a decent burial (114). Then the criminals make 'a hollow' in the same hall to put their treasure in (115). They are taking much more care of that than they are with the remains of a human being, who has done nothing wrong.

There is some justice, as the four conspirators are 'arrested as the murderers of Achmet' at the end of the Indian Rebellion (116). However, 'not a word about the jewels came out at the trial, for the rajah had been deposed and driven out of India' (116). Hence, the treasure still has not been recovered by the authorities, who are unaware of its existence.

Small bides his time as a prisoner and is eventually relocated to 'Blair Island in the Andamans' (117). While there, he talks to Major Sholto, who is 'a ruined man' following some heavy losses while playing cards (118). Small asks Sholto whether handing over the 'hidden treasure' will get his 'sentence shortened' (118).

Sholto brings Captain Morstan to Small and asks him to repeat the story. Sholto decides it is 'a private concern' rather than a governmental matter (119) and agrees that he and the captain should share a fifth of the treasure, which comes 'to fifty thousand apiece' (120).

Once Small gives Sholto and Morstan the maps, the Major goes off 'to India but' never comes 'back again' (121). Although it's a case of the pot calling the kettle black, Small calls Sholto a 'villain' (121).

Thereafter, Small is completely consumed with thoughts of vengeance as he admits that 'even the Agra treasure had come to be a smaller thing' in his mind compared to 'the slaying of Sholto' (122).

Around that time, Small befriends a 'little Andaman Islander', who is 'sick to death', called 'Tonga' (122). Small nurses Tonga back to health, who ferries him away from the island.

Once Small returns to England with Tonga, he makes 'friends with someone who' can help him (123). He won't 'name no names', so this part of the account remains a mystery, allowing the reader to guess (123).

Alluding to the infamous Victorian freak shows, Small reveals that he profited from 'exhibiting poor Tonga at fair and other such places as the black cannibal' (124). This shows that Small is no stranger to exploiting others for his own gain.

Small describes Tonga 'as proud as a peacock', after the murder of Bartholomew (124). This suggests again, that he sees the Islander as little more than a crude animal. He goes on to describe him as 'a bloodthirsty little imp', which again reveals how little regard he has for him (125).

After Small finishes his story and heads for prison, Watson reveals his engagement to Miss Morstan. Holmes gives out 'a most dismal groan', which shows how selfish he is (126). Holmes says: 'I really cannot congratulate you' (126). He explains to Watson that 'whatever is emotional is opposed to that true cold reason' which he places above all things (126). Once again, the reader is reminded to align reason with Holmes and emotion with Watson.

The end of the story sees Holmes return to his drug of choice, cocaine. However, before he does that he surmises that Small's 'confederate in the house' was probably Lal Rao and, thinking of himself, quotes Goethe (127). The translation of the quotation is: 'Nature, alas, made only one being out of you although there was material for a good man and a rogue'. These words sum up Holmes's 'Jeckyl and Hyde' nature and indicate he could have ended up as a devious criminal had he not become a detective instead.

CLOUD 9 – 'THE SIGN OF FOUR' STUDY GUIDE

AQA-style Specimen Assessment Material 1:
Starting with this extract, explore how Conan Doyle presents criminals in *The Sign of Four*.
Write about:
• how does Conan Doyle present the criminal in this extract
• how does Conan Doyle present criminals in the novel as a whole.

EXTRACT

Sir Arthur Conan Doyle: The Sign of Four
Read the following extract from Chapter 11 of The Sign of Four and then answer the question.
In this extract, Holmes is about to talk to Jonathan Small, who has just been arrested for his part in the death of Bartholomew Sholto and the theft of the Agra Treasure. The extract is important for it reveals contemporary attitudes towards criminals.

Our captive sat in the cabin opposite to the iron box which he had done so much and waited so long to gain. He was a sunburned, reckless-eyed fellow, with a net-work of lines and wrinkles all over his mahogany features, which told of a hard, open-air life. There was a singular prominence about his bearded chin which marked a man who was not to be easily turned from his purpose. His age may have been fifty or thereabouts, for his black, curly hair was thickly shot with grey. His face in repose was not an unpleasing one, though his heavy brows and aggressive chin gave him, as I had lately seen, a terrible expression when moved to anger. He sat now with his handcuffed hands upon his lap, and his head sunk upon his breast, while he looked with his keen, twinkling eyes at the box which had been the cause of his ill-doings. It seemed to me that there was more sorrow than anger in his rigid and contained countenance. Once he looked up at me with a gleam of something like humour in his eyes.

"Well, Jonathan Small," said Holmes, lighting a cigar, "I am sorry that it has come to this."

Comment [JB(]: AO2 – The word 'captive' reminds us that Small has sacrificed his freedom in order to try to

Comment [JB(]: AO1 – Small is positioned next to the box that is expected to contain the treasure. The

Comment [JB(]: AO2 – The repetition of the word 'so' gives the reader gets the sense that criminals can be incredibly

Comment [JB(]: AO1 – If eyes are the windows to the soul, the 'reckless-eyed' Small would be impossible to trust

Comment [JB(]: AO2 – The word 'network' reminds readers of how criminals need to establish and maintain

Comment [JB(]: AO1 – The message here is crime does not pay. All it has led to, in the case of Small, is 'a hard, open-

Comment [JB(]: AO1 – Small's determination is not in question. However, he has put it to the wrong use

Comment [JB(]: AO3 – These physical features tie in with the popular Victorian pseudo-science of physiognomy, which

Comment [JB(]: AO1 – The writer shows how awful it is for criminals when they are caught, conveying the message again

Comment [JB(]: AO2 – The description of his eyes as 'keen' and 'twinkling' imply intelligence married with greed, as the

Comment [JB(]: AO1 – The writer shows that the criminal is sad, but we cannot be sure about why. It could be that it

Comment [JB(]: AO1 – We get the impression that the narrator cannot understand the criminal mind, as he is

"And so am I, sir," he answered, frankly. "I don't believe that I can
swing over the job. I give you my word on the book that I never
raised hand against Mr. Sholto. It was that little hell-hound Tonga
who shot one of his cursed darts into him. I had no part in it, sir. I
was as grieved as if it had been my blood-relation. I welted the little
devil with the slack end of the rope for it, but it was done, and I
could not undo it again."

AQA-style Specimen Assessment Material 2:

**Starting with this extract, explore how Conan Doyle presents
women in *The Sign of Four*.**
Write about:
• **how does Conan Doyle present women in this extract**
• **how does Conan Doyle present women in the novel as a whole.**

EXTRACT

Sir Arthur Conan Doyle: The Sign of Four
Read the following extract from Chapter 7 of The Sign of
Four and then answer the question.
In this extract, Watson is escorting Mary Morstan to her place
of work and residence. She is employed as a governess by
Mrs Cecil Forrester (who, interestingly, is known formally by
her husband's first name). The extract is important for it
reveals contemporary attitudes towards women.

It was nearly two o'clock when we reached Mrs. Cecil Forrester's.
The servants had retired hours ago, but Mrs. Forrester had been so
interested by the strange message which Miss Morstan had received
that she had sat up in the hope of her return. She opened the door
herself, a middle-aged, graceful woman, and it gave me joy to see
how tenderly her arm stole round the other's waist and how motherly
was the voice in which she greeted her. She was clearly no mere paid
dependant, but an honored friend. I was introduced, and Mrs.
Forrester earnestly begged me to step in and tell her our adventures. I
explained, however, the importance of my errand, and promised

Comment [JB(]: AO1 – Despite his
capture, Small is respectful to Holmes.
More cynical readers may think it is in the
hope that he will get a lighter sentence

Comment [JB(]: AO2 – The alliterative
'hell-hound' emphasises how evil Tonga is
in Small's eyes. However, hounds are
known for their loyalty, which is not being

Comment [JB(]: AO1 – The idea of
honour amongst thieves is lost on Small,
who immediately tells Holmes that Tonga
is the murderer. The reader may find it

Comment [JB(]: AO1 – Although she is
Mary Mostan's employer, Mrs Forrester is
presented as homely and caring, staying
awake later than usual to greet her

Comment [JB(]: AO1 – Mrs Forrester
has even allowed the servants to go to
bed, and has gone to considerable effort
to wait for Mary's return. She is portrayed

Comment [JB(]: AO2 – The adverbs
'tenderly' and 'motherly' add to the
impression that Mrs Forrester is a kind,
caring and warm person.

Comment [JB(]: AO1 – The relationship
between the two women is much more
than simply a working arrangement.
Although, Mary works for Mrs Forrester

Comment [JB(]: AO1 – Mrs Forrester is
portrayed as a welcoming hostess to
Watson, whom she has never met before.
This makes her appear very trusting

Comment [JB(]: AO1 – The implication
here is that men's work is more important
than women's, although Watson
modestly describes his job as 'errand'.

faithfully to call and report any progress which we might make with the case. As we drove away I stole a glance back, and I still seem to see that little group on the step, the two graceful, clinging figures, the half opened door, the hall light shining through stained glass, the barometer, and the bright stair-rods. It was soothing to catch even that passing glimpse of a tranquil English home in the midst of the wild, dark business which had absorbed us.

AQA-style Specimen Assessment Material 3:

Starting with this extract, explore how Conan Doyle presents Watson in *The Sign of Four*.
Write about:
• **how does Conan Doyle present Watson in this extract**
• **how does Conan Doyle present Watson in the novel as a whole.**

EXTRACT

Sir Arthur Conan Doyle: The Sign of Four
Read the following extract from Chapter 7 of The Sign of Four and then answer the question.
In this extract, Watson is following Holmes instructions to escort Mary Morstan home, not long after the discovery of the murdered Batholomew Sholto. The extract is important for it shows how Watson 's emotional involvement in the case gives it a different hue to Holmes, who sees 'a client as a mere unit '.

The police had brought a cab with them, and in this I escorted Miss Morstan back to her home. After the angelic fashion of women, she had borne trouble with a calm face as long as there was some one weaker than herself to support, and I had found her bright and placid by the side of the frightened housekeeper. In the cab, however, she first turned faint, and then burst into a passion of weeping,—so sorely had she been tried by the adventures of the night. She has told me since that she thought me cold and distant upon that journey. She little guessed the struggle within my breast, or the effort of self-restraint which held me back. My sympathies and my love went out to her, even as my hand had in the garden. I felt that years of the

Comment [JB(]: AO3 – The image of two helpless women in front of a house holding each other desperately is typical

Comment [JB(]: AO2 – The writer uses religious imagery to describe the women. The scene gains an almost holy light as

Comment [JB(]: AO2 – The juxtaposition of light and dark here flatters these gentlewomen, who seem to be located in

Comment [JB(]: AO1 – By applying the word 'angelic' to women in general, Watson conveys the idea that he thinks all

Comment [JB(]: AO1 – Watson's fixation on Mary is obvious, as he observes and admires her strong, but feminine

Comment [JB(]: AO1 – Once again, Watson conveys his admiration for Mary, who he believes can be strong when she

Comment [JB(]: AO2 – The writer uses the soft sound of sibilance to show how Watson is ready to excuse Mary's sobbing

Comment [JB(]: AO1 – Watson's revelation that 'she has told me since' reveals that he has maintained some of

Comment [JB(]: AO2 – The metaphor of the 'struggle within' Watson's 'breast' reminds us that this is a matter of the

Comment [JB(]: AO2 – The personification of 'sympathies and love' make it appear as if Watson is completely

Comment [JB(]: AO1 – Watson reminds us that he has already made physical contact with Mary. He clearly is losing the

conventionalities of life could not teach me to know her sweet, brave nature as had this one day of strange experiences. Yet there were two thoughts which sealed the words of affection upon my lips. She was weak and helpless, shaken in mind and nerve. It was to take her at a disadvantage to obtrude love upon her at such a time. Worse still, she was rich. If Holmes's researches were successful, she would be an heiress. Was it fair, was it honorable, that a half-pay surgeon should take such advantage of an intimacy which chance had brought about? Might she not look upon me as a mere vulgar fortuneseeker? I could not bear to risk that such a thought should cross her mind. This Agra treasure intervened like an impassable barrier between us.

AQA-style Specimen Assessment Material 4: 'Jonathan Small is a totally unsympathetic character.'
Starting with this extract, how does Conan Doyle present the character of Thaddeus Sholto?
Write about:
• how Conan Doyle presents Thaddeus Sholto in this extract
• how Conan Doyle presents Thaddeus Sholto in the novel as a whole.

EXTRACT

Sir Arthur Conan Doyle: The Sign of Four
Read the following extract from Chapter 4 of The Sign of Four and then answer the question.
In this extract, Holmes, Watson and Mary Morstan meet and speak to Thaddeus Sholto in his not-so-humble abode. They have travelled through London to get here from the Lyceum Theatre and now they are hoping that Thaddeus, whom they have just met, will help them unravel the mystery. The extract is important as we gain insight into Watson's view of Thaddeus.

"Mr. Thaddeus Sholto," said the little man, still jerking and smiling. "That is my name. You are
Miss Morstan, of course. And these gentlemen—"

Comment [JB(]: AO2 – The use of hyperbole implies that Watson is ready to fall in love in 'one day'. He seems to believe that because of all the 'strange experiences', he has learned as much about Mary as if he had been with her for a number of 'years'.

Comment [JB(]: AO2 – The 'two thoughts' are personified, which gives them even greater importance.

Comment [JB(]: AO3 – Watson wants to a Victorian gentleman in every sense of the word. Therefore to 'obtrude' or force love on a vulnerable woman is anathema to him.

Comment [JB(]: AO3 – In Victorian times, people were supposed to marry others in a similar socio-economic position. If Mary becomes rich, Watson cannot marry her unless he and she are

Comment [JB(]: AO2 – Using a series of rhetorical questions, Watson persuades himself that he is unworthy of Mary's hand in marriage. This makes him appear as an honourable Victorian gentleman to

Comment [JB(]: AO2 – The simile of the 'impassable barrier' makes the reader realise how important honour and convention is to Watson. While he is unquestionably a decent man, it appears

Comment [JB(]: AO2 – The –ing form of both verbs makes it appear that Thaddeus is continually 'jerking and smiling'. It appears that he of a nervous disposition.

"This is Mr. Sherlock Holmes, and this is Dr. Watson."

"A doctor, eh?" cried he, much excited. "Have you your stethoscope? Might I ask you—would you have the kindness? I have grave doubts as to my mitral valve, if you would be so very good. The aortic I may rely upon, but I should value your opinion upon the mitral."

I listened to his heart, as requested, but was unable to find anything amiss, save indeed that he was in an ecstasy of fear, for he shivered from head to foot. "It appears to be normal," I said. "You have no cause for uneasiness."

"You will excuse my anxiety, Miss Morstan," he remarked, airily. "I am a great sufferer, and I have long had suspicions as to that valve. I am delighted to hear that they are unwarranted. Had your father, Miss Morstan, refrained from throwing a strain upon his heart, he might have been alive now."

I could have struck the man across the face, so hot was I at this callous and off-hand reference to so delicate a matter. Miss Morstan sat down, and her face grew white to the lips. "I knew in my heart that he was dead," said she.

"I can give you every information," said he, "and, what is more, I can do you justice; and I will, too, whatever Brother Bartholomew may say. I am so glad to have your friends here, not only as an escort to you, but also as witnesses to what I am about to do and say. The three of us can show a bold front to Brother Bartholomew. But let us have no outsiders,—no police or officials. We can settle everything satisfactorily among ourselves, without any interference. Nothing would annoy Brother Bartholomew more than any publicity." He sat down upon a low settee and blinked at us inquiringly with his weak, watery blue eyes.

AQA-style Specimen Assessment Material 5:

Comment [JB(]: AO1 – We quickly discover Thaddeus is a hypochondriac, as he immediately wants Watson to examine him.
AO2 – Thaddeus uses technical language,

Comment [JB(]: AO2 – The word 'ecstasy' is usually a positive word, where 'fear' is anything but. Therefore, this works an oxymoron to show how confused Thaddeus. On the one hand, he

Comment [JB(]: AO1 – As we see the action mostly through Watson's eyes, we are unlikely to warm to Thaddeus's character, especially after this outburst, which makes him appear insensitive.

Comment [JB(]: AO1 – Thaddeus appears to be much weaker than his brother, if we believe his testimony.

Comment [JB(]: AO2 – The use of negative language shows how Thaddeus is scared of the law and anything outside of his sphere of influence.

Comment [JB(]: AO2 – The fact that Thaddeus is sitting on a 'low' settee implies that he could be immoral, as he is positioned nearer the devil that God.
AO3 – His moral could be questionable by

Comment [JB(]: AO2 – Thaddeus appears to be a physically fragile character, judging by his 'weak, watery' eyes.

Starting with this extract, explore the ideas conveyed by Conan Doyle about Holmes's character through his dealings with 'ordinary people' in *The Sign of Four*.
Write about:
• how does Conan Doyle convey ideas about Holmes's character through his dealings with 'ordinary people' in this extract
• how does Conan Doyle convey ideas about Holmes's character through his dealings with 'ordinary people' in the novel as a whole.

EXTRACT

Sir Arthur Conan Doyle: The Sign of Four
Read the following extract from Chapter 8 of The Sign of Four and then answer the question.

In this extract, Holmes is talking to Mrs Smith, Mordecai's wife, about the 'Aurora' and her husband. The extract is important for it reveals contemporary attitudes towards the lower classes.

But, my dear Mrs. Smith," said Holmes, shrugging his shoulders, "You are frightening yourself about nothing. How could you possibly tell that it was the wooden-legged man who came in the night? I don't quite understand how you can be so sure."

"His voice, sir. I knew his voice, which is kind o' thick and foggy. He tapped at the winder,—about three it would be. 'Show a leg, matey,' says he: 'time to turn out guard.' My old man woke up Jim,—that's my eldest,—and away they went, without so much as a word to me. I could hear the wooden leg clackin' on the stones."

"And was this wooden-legged man alone?"

"Couldn't say, I am sure, sir. I didn't hear no one else."

Comment [JB(]: AO1 – Holmes's adopts a benign but patronising tone with a working-class woman.

Comment [JB(]: AO2 – Holmes uses a rhetorical question to show how ridiculous Mrs Smith is being.

Comment [JB(]: AO2 – The author writes phonetically here to show Mrs Smith's accent and imply a lack of education.
AO3 – Free elementary education was only provided from 1891, the year after 'The Sign of Four' was published.

Comment [JB(]: AO2 – The writer portrays Mrs Smith as uneducated through her lack of grammar and the use of a double negative.

"I am sorry, Mrs. Smith, for I wanted a steam launch, and I have heard good reports of the—Let
me see, what is her name?"

"The Aurora, sir."

"Ah! She's not that old green launch with a yellow line, very broad in the beam?"

"No, indeed. She's as trim a little thing as any on the river. She's been fresh painted, black with
two red streaks."

"Thanks. I hope that you will hear soon from Mr. Smith. I am going down the river, and if I should see anything of the Aurora I shall let him know that you are uneasy. A black funnel, you say?"

"No, sir. Black with a white band."

"Ah, of course. It was the sides which were black. Good-morning, Mrs. Smith.—There is a boatman
here with a wherry, Watson. We shall take it and cross the river.

"The main thing with people of that sort," said Holmes, as we sat in the sheets of the wherry, "is never to let them think that their information can be of the slightest importance to you. If you do, they will instantly shut up like an oyster. If you listen to them under protest, as it were, you are very likely to get what you want."

AQA-style Specimen Assessment Material 6:
Starting with this extract, explore the ideas conveyed about the media and the police by Conan Doyle in _The Sign of Four_.
Write about:
• **how does Conan Doyle convey ideas about the media and the police in this extract**
• **how does Conan Doyle convey ideas about the media and the police in the novel as a whole.**

EXTRACT

Comment [JB(]: AO3 – The class system is apparent, as Mrs Smith addresses Holmes as 'sir', whereas he does not refer to her as 'madam' or 'miss'.

Comment [JB(]: AO2 – Mrs Smith continues to use poor grammar, this time not using an adverb correctly. This again portrays her as poorly educated.

Comment [JB(]: AO2 – Holmes's speech includes a semi-colon and lack the contractions that Mrs Smith's dialogue contains. The juxtaposition of the two characters makes Holmes seems superior and well educated in comparison to her.

Comment [JB(]: AO3 – The wherry was evolving into a gentleman's form of river transport in the Victorian era. They were later called skiffs. Holmes shows how different he is to the working-class Mrs Smith, who would not be able to afford this mode of transport.

Comment [JB(]: AO1 – Holmes is extremely condescending, dismissive and ready to generalise about the working-classes, when he speaks to Watson (who is from the same social class).

Comment [JB(]: AO2 – The use of the simile likens the working-classes to the food they used to eat in the nineteenth-century. It has the effect of making them seem cheap and easy to buy, while also suggesting that they will not open their

Sir Arthur Conan Doyle: The Sign of Four
Read the following extract from Chapter 8 of The Sign of
Four and then answer the question.
In this extract, Holmes and Watson are enjoying breakfast
together after the successive excitements of the night before.
The extract is important for it reveals contemporary attitudes
towards the media and the police.

"Here it is," said he, laughing, and pointing to an open newspaper.
"The energetic Jones and the
ubiquitous reporter have fixed it up between them. But you have had
enough of the case. Better have
your ham and eggs first."

I took the paper from him and read the short notice, which was
headed "Mysterious Business at Upper Norwood."

"About twelve o'clock last night," said the Standard, "Mr.
Bartholomew Sholto, of Pondicherry Lodge, Upper Norwood, was
found dead in his room under circumstances which point to foul play.
As far as we can learn, no actual traces of violence were found upon
Mr. Sholto's person, but a valuable collection of Indian gems which
the deceased gentleman had inherited from his father has been
carried off. The discovery was first made by Mr. Sherlock Holmes
and Dr. Watson, who had called at the house with Mr. Thaddeus
Sholto, brother of the deceased. By a singular piece of good fortune,
Mr. Athelney Jones, the well-known member of the detective police
force, happened to be at the Norwood Police Station, and was on the
ground within half an hour of the first alarm. His trained and
experienced faculties were at once directed towards the detection of
the criminals, with the gratifying result that the brother, Thaddeus
Sholto, has already been arrested, together with the housekeeper,
Mrs. Bernstone, an Indian butler named Lal Rao, and a porter, or
gatekeeper, named McMurdo. It is quite certain that the thief or
thieves were well acquainted with the house, for Mr. Jones's well-
known technical knowledge and his powers of minute observation
have enabled him to prove conclusively that the miscreants could not
have entered by the door or by the window, but must have made their

Comment [JB(]: AO1 – Holmes's
cynicism towards both professions is
evident in his ironic use of the word
'energetic' and 'ubiquitous'. The unfit

Comment [JB(]: AO1 – The repetition of
Jones's favourite word 'business' shows
that the policeman has had a hand in
coming up with the headline. The

Comment [JB(]: AO1 – Holmes and
Watson removed the poison dart from
the scene of the crime, but the police
should have noticed a puncture mark in

Comment [JB(]: AO1 – Like Jones, the
reporter believes that 'good fortune' or
luck is important when it comes to solving
crimes.

Comment [JB(]: AO2 – The
complimentary adjectives 'trained and
experienced' add to the idea that the
reporter is writing this for the benefit of

Comment [JB(]: AO1 – The
incompetence of both the media and the
police is evident here, as the reporter
calls the arrests 'gratifying'. The truth is

Comment [JB(]: AO1 – Once again, the
report flatters Jones. Instead of to the
policeman, these words could be rightly
applied to Holmes.

Comment [JB(]: AO2 – It is ironic that
the reporter thinks Jones has proved
anything 'conclusively', when he has in
fact done nothing of the sort. The word is

way across the roof of the building, and so through a trap-door into a room which communicated with that in which the body was found. This fact, which has been very clearly made out, proves conclusively that it was no mere haphazard burglary. The prompt and energetic action of the officers of the law shows the great advantage of the presence on such occasions of a single vigorous and masterful mind. We cannot but think that it supplies an argument to those who wish to see our detectives more decentralized, and so brought into closer and more effective touch with the cases which it is their duty to investigate."

Comment [JB(]: AO2 – As readers, we know that only Holmes has a 'masterful mind', so the alliteration works to add unintended humour to the journalist's report.

Comment [JB(]: AO3 – The journalist is voicing the concern that as Britain seemingly became smaller, due to the improvement in the country's infrastructure, there was increasing pressure to centralise public services. Unfortunately, the reporter's assertion that Jones is living proof of how efficient local police inspectors can benefit the community is wrong.

Comment [JB(]: AO1 – The fact that Mary Morstan can say goodbye in French makes her appear refined, which would make her a worthy love interest for Watson to pursue.

AQA-style Specimen Assessment Material 7:
Starting with this extract, explore how Conan Doyle presents the theme of love and romance in *The Sign of Four*.
Write about:
• **how does Conan Doyle present the theme of love and romance in this extract**
• **how does Conan Doyle present the theme of love and romance in the novel as a whole.**

EXTRACT

Sir Arthur Conan Doyle: The Sign of Four
Read the following extract from Chapter 2 of The Sign of Four and then answer the question.
In this extract, Watson has the opportunity to speak to Holmes about Mary Morstan, who is just leaving 221B Baker Street. The extract is important for it explores the theme of love and romance, showing that just because the emotional Watson is attracted to her and sees her as the ideal Victorian woman, it does not follow that his close friend, Holmes, will also find her attractive.

"Au revoir," said our visitor, and, with a bright, kindly glance from one to the other of us, she replaced her pearl-box in her bosom and hurried away. Standing at the window, I watched her walking briskly down the street, until the grey turban and white feather were but a speck in the sombre crowd.

"What a very attractive woman!" I exclaimed, turning to my companion.

He had lit his pipe again, and was leaning back with drooping eyelids. "Is she?" he said, languidly.
"I did not observe."

"You really are an automaton,—a calculating machine!" I cried. "There is something positively inhuman in you at times."

He smiled gently. "It is of the first importance," he said, "not to allow your judgment to be biased by personal qualities. A client is to me a mere unit,—a factor in a problem. The emotional qualities are antagonistic to clear reasoning. I assure you that the most winning woman I ever knew was hanged for poisoning three little children for their insurance-money, and the most repellant man of my acquaintance is a philanthropist who has spent nearly a quarter of a million upon the London poor."

"In this case, however—"

"I never make exceptions. An exception disproves the rule. Have you ever had occasion to study character in handwriting? What do you make of this fellow's scribble?"

AQA-style Specimen Assessment Material 8: 'Jonathan Small is a totally unsympathetic character.'
Starting with this extract, how far do you agree with this statement?
Write about:
• **how Conan Doyle presents Jonathan Small in this extract**
• **how Conan Doyle presents Jonathan Small in the novel as a whole.**

Comment [JB(]: AO1 – Mary does not seem to want to draw attention to herself, which is why she walks 'briskly'

Comment [JB(]: AO2 – Watson refers to her as 'a speck', which implies that she can disappear quite quickly from his life

Comment [JB(]: Structurally, the writer uses an exclamation mark to highlight how bowled over Holmes is by Mary

Comment [JB(]: AO1 – Holmes shows how bored with love and romance he is in his reaction to Watson's exclamation.

Comment [JB(]: AO3 – The Victorian battle between rationalism (represented by Holmes) and sentimentalism

Comment [JB(]: AO1 – Holmes seems to be warning Watson not to fall in love. As a rationalist, Holmes does not believe that

Comment [JB(]: AO3 – Holmes begins to spells out the case for rationalism over emotional sentimentalism, explaining that

Comment [JB(]: AO2 – The superlative 'most winning' is emphasised with the alliterative 'woman' to make Holmes

Comment [JB(]: AO2 – Another superlative 'most repellant' is used to describe a generous 'philanthropist'. By

Comment [JB(]: AO2 – The writer uses the interrupted dialogue between Holmes and Watson to show how the cynical

Comment [JB(]: AO1 – Holmes shifts the focus back to the detection of crime, thereby prematurely ending Watson's

EXTRACT

Sir Arthur Conan Doyle: The Sign of Four

Read the following extract from Chapter 12 of The Sign of Four and then answer the question.

In this extract, Jonathan Small is telling Holmes, Watson and Athelney Jones about the murder of the 'pretended merchant', Achmet, and how the treasure, which now lies at the bottom of the Thames, was originally stolen by the members of 'The Sign of Four' (Small, Mahomet Singh, Abdullah Khan and Dost Akba). The extract is important as we gain insight into Watson's point of view of Small, for a brief moment here, in this break in the embedded narrative.

You see, gentlemen, that I am keeping my promise. I am telling you every work of the business just exactly as it happened, whether it is in my favor or not."

He stopped, and held out his manacled hands for the whiskey-and-water which Holmes had brewed for him. For myself, I confess that I had now conceived the utmost horror of the man, not only for this cold-blooded business in which he had been concerned, but even more for the somewhat flippant and careless way in which he narrated it. Whatever punishment was in store for him, I felt that he might expect no sympathy from me. Sherlock Holmes and Jones sat with their hands upon their knees, deeply interested in the story, but with the same disgust written upon their faces. He may have observed it, for there was a touch of defiance in his voice and manner as he proceeded.

"It was all very bad, no doubt," said he. "I should like to know how many fellows in my shoes would have refused a share of this loot when they knew that they would have their throats cut for their pains. Besides, it was my life or his when once he was in the fort. If he had got out, the whole business would come to light, and I should have been court-martialled and shot as likely as not; for people were not very lenient at a time like that."

"Go on with your story," said Holmes, shortly.

Comment [JB(]: AO1 - As narrator, Small is attempting to curry favour with his listeners, by reminding them how he is

Comment [JB(]: AO3 – In keeping with the generic conventions of detective fiction, the criminal has admitted that

Comment [JB(]: AO1 – It seems as if Holmes has some sympathy for Small, or at least for his story, given that he is

Comment [JB(]: AO3 – The words 'utmost horror' make his heinous crimes fit into the genre of the gothic, in

Comment [JB(]: AO2 – The use of hackneyed figurative language makes it seem as if Watson is a typical Victorian

Comment [JB(]: AO1 – Watson is particularly disgusted by Small's seeming lack of remorse and is unimpressed by the

Comment [JB(]: AO1 – Despite their professional curiosity, even Holmes and Jones are disgusted by Small's story.

Comment [JB(]: AO2 – The abstract noun 'defiance' implies a lack of remorse. If that is the case, it is very difficult for any

Comment [JB(]: AO2 – The use of a rhetorical question in Small's narrative makes him appear persuasive. It appears

Comment [JB(]: AO1 – In his matter-of-fact way, Small makes it sound as if it were his life or the merchant's. It appears

AQA-style Specimen Assessment Material 9:
Starting with this extract, explore how Conan Doyle build up an atmosphere of fear and terror in *The Sign of Four*.
Write about:
• **how does Conan Doyle build up an atmosphere of fear and terror present Watson in this extract**
• **how does Conan Doyle build up an atmosphere of fear and terror in the novel as a whole.**

EXTRACT

Sir Arthur Conan Doyle: The Sign of Four
Read the following extract from Chapter 5 of The Sign of Four and then answer the question.
In this extract, Holmes, Watson, Mary Morstan and Thaddeus Sholto have arrived at Pondicherry Lodge to see Thaddeus's brother, Batholomew. Holmes has just looked through the keyhole into Bartholomew's room and looks shocked by what he has just seen. The extract is important for it is one of the most horrific moments in the narrative.

"There is something devilish in this, Watson," said he, more moved than I had ever before seen him. "What do you make of it?"

I stooped to the hole, and recoiled in horror. Moonlight was streaming into the room, and it was bright with a vague and shifty radiance. Looking straight at me, and suspended, as it were, in the air, for all beneath was in shadow, there hung a face—the very face of our companion Thaddeus. There was the same high, shining head, the same circular bristle of red hair, the same bloodless countenance. The features were set, however, in a horrible smile, a fixed and unnatural grin, which in that still and moonlit room was more jarring to the nerves than any scowl or contortion. So like was the face to that of our little friend that I looked round at him to make sure that he was indeed with us. Then I recalled to mind that he had mentioned to us that his brother and he were twins.

Comment [JB(): AO3 – The adjective 'devilish' connects with the genre of gothic horror, as it is almost as if Holmes suspects a supernatural force is at work. Being the rational person that he is,

Comment [JB(): AO1 – The verb 'recoiled' implies that the shock of what is seen is extremely horrific. At this stage, it is fear of the unknown for the reader, as the narrator has not yet disclosed what

Comment [JB(): AO2 – The personification of the 'moonlight' makes the night seem all the more dangerous. The fact that it is 'streaming into the room' makes it appear as if it is powerful

Comment [JB(): AO1 – Through the setting, the writer conveys the unknown. It is difficult to pin down what exactly has happened with only the 'vague and shifty radiance' of the moonlight to operate in.

Comment [JB(): AO2 – The words 'suspended', 'shadow' and 'hung' connote death by hanging, which to the fear and terror which have already been created in the extract.

Comment [JB(): AO3 – Bartholomew is the gothic double of his brother, Thaddeus. This also adds to the fear factor, as these identical twins give a sense of the uncanny, which links to the

Comment [JB(): AO2 – Using a triplet, the writer conveys the idea of how atrocious the dead body looks: its grin is 'horrible', 'fixed' and 'unnatural'. This adds tension heightening the horror and

CLOUD 9 – 'THE SIGN OF FOUR' STUDY GUIDE

"This is terrible!" I said to Holmes. "What is to be done?"

"The door must come down," he answered, and, springing against it, he put all his weight upon the
lock. It creaked and groaned, but did not yield. Together we flung ourselves upon it once more, and this time it gave way with a sudden snap, and we found ourselves within Bartholomew Sholto's chamber.

Comment [JB(]: AO1 – Watson's reaction to the horror is ask Holmes what should done. Although Watson has been involved in a war in Afghanistan, the atrocity that has met his eyes appears to be far worse.

Comment [JB(]: AO2 – The writer uses onomatopoeia to add drama to breaking in of the door. The noise of the 'snap' makes this appear to herald another moment of horror as they find themselves in Bartholomew's bedroom.

Comment [JB(]: AO3 – The Andaman Islands were colonised by Britain and were used as a penal colony following the Indian Rebellion of 1857. The British Empire is so large than even Holmes has to look in encyclopaedias to find out more information. This shows an attitude of fascination for far-off places.

AQA-style Specimen Assessment Material 10:
Starting with this extract, explore the ideas conveyed about the British Empire by Conan Doyle in *The Sign of Four*.
Write about:
• **how does Conan Doyle convey ideas about the British Empire in this extract**
• **how does Conan Doyle convey ideas about the British Empire in the novel as a whole.**

EXTRACT

Sir Arthur Conan Doyle: The Sign of Four
Read the following extract from Chapter 8 of The Sign of Four and then answer the question.
In this extract, Holmes and Watson are discussing the murder of Bartholomew. Holmes is just about to look in an encyclopaedia to find out more background information on the racial identity of Jonathan Small's associate, who fired a dart from a blow pipe into Bartholomew's neck. The extract is important for it reveals the some of the prevalent attitudes of the Victorian age.

He stretched his hand up, and took down a bulky volume from the shelf. "This is the first volume
of a gazetteer which is now being published. It may be looked upon as the very latest authority.
What have we here? 'Andaman Islands, situated 340 miles to the north of Sumatra, in the Bay of

Bengal.' Hum! hum! What's all this? Moist climate, coral reefs, sharks, Port Blair, convict-barracks, Rutland Island, cottonwoods—Ah, here we are. 'The aborigines of the Andaman Islands may perhaps
claim the distinction of being the smallest race upon this earth, though some anthropologists prefer the Bushmen of Africa, the Digger Indians of America, and the Terra del Fuegians. The average height is rather below four feet, although many full-grown adults may be found who are very much smaller than this. They are a fierce, morose, and intractable people, though capable of forming most devoted friendships when their confidence has once been gained.' Mark that, Watson. Now, then, listen to this. 'They are naturally hideous, having large, misshapen heads, small, fierce eyes, and distorted features. Their feet and hands, however, are remarkably small. So intractable and fierce are they that all the efforts of the British official have failed to win them over in any degree. They have always been a terror to shipwrecked crews, braining the survivors with their stone-headed clubs, or shooting them with their poisoned arrows. These massacres are invariably concluded by a cannibal feast.' Nice, amiable people, Watson! If this fellow had been left to his own unaided devices this affair might have taken an even more ghastly turn. I fancy that, even as it is, Jonathan Small would give a good deal not to have employed him."

AQA-style Specimen Assessment Material 11:
Starting with this extract, explore how Conan Doyle presents the theme of greed and avarice in *The Sign of Four*.
Write about:
• how does Conan Doyle present the theme of greed and avarice in this extract
• how does Conan Doyle present the theme of greed and avarice in the novel as a whole.

EXTRACT

Sir Arthur Conan Doyle: The Sign of Four
Read the following extract from Chapter 4 of The Sign of Four and then answer the question.

Comment [JB(]: AO2 – The writer uses triplets to show how dangerous the people are that are native to the Andamans. Each adjective is negative,

Comment [JB(]: AO1 – A positive generalisation indicates that Andaman Islanders can be befriended, if approached with caution. Despite this

Comment [JB(]: AO1 – The description matches the narrator's report on how Tonga looks later in the novella.
AO3 – Many Victorians believed in the

Comment [JB(]: AO1 – The word 'efforts' implies the British have tried very hard to 'win them over', but it has all been to no avail.

Comment [JB(]: AO2 – The –ing form of the verbs 'braining' or 'shooting' makes it appear that these activities are still continuing.

Comment [JB(]: AO1 – These horrific details paint a vivid and detailed pictures of wild and dangerous Andaman Islanders, who seem ready to eat human

Comment [JB(]: AO1 – Here, Holmes uncharacteristically jumps to conclusions. It does not necessarily follow that the Andaman Islander is more vicious than

Comment [JB(]: AO1 – This makes it sounds as if Jonathan Small's biggest crime is to have employed him. We can only assume that partly because Small is

In this extract, through Thaddeus's embedded narrative, we hear the last words of his father, Major John Sholto, on his death bed. The extract is important for it explores the theme of avarice, implying also that crime does not pay.

" 'I have only one thing,' he [Major John Sholto] said, 'which weighs upon my mind at this supreme moment. It is my treatment of poor Morstan's orphan [Mary]. The cursed greed which has been my besetting sin through life has withheld from her the treasure, half at least of which should have been hers. And yet I have made no use of it myself.—so blind and foolish a thing is avarice. The mere feeling of possession has been so dear to me that I could not bear to share it with another. See that chaplet dipped with pearls beside the quinine-bottle. Even that I could not bear to part with, although I had got it out with the design of sending it to her. You, my sons, will give her a fair share of the Agra treasure. But send her nothing—not even the chaplet—until I am gone. After all, men have been as bad as this and have recovered.

" 'I will tell you how Morstan died,' he continued. 'He had suffered for years from a weak heart, but he concealed it from every one. I alone knew it. When in India, he and I, through a remarkable chain of circumstances, came into possession of a considerable treasure. I brought it over to England, and on the night of Morstan's arrival he came straight over here to claim his share. He walked over from the station, and was admitted by my faithful Lal Chowdar, who is now dead. Morstan and I had a difference of opinion as to the division of the treasure, and we came to heated words. Morstan had sprung out of his chair in a paroxysm of anger, when he suddenly pressed his hand to his side, his face turned a dusky hue, and he fell backwards, cutting his head against the corner of the treasure-chest. When I stooped over him I found, to my horror, that he was dead.

AQA-style Specimen Assessment Material 12:
Starting with this extract, explore how Conan Doyle contrasts the methods and character of Athelney Jones with Sherlock Holmes.
Write about:

Comment [JB(]: AO2 – The personification of the word 'greed'

Comment [JB(]: AO1 – Major Sholto, at least, admits that 'half' of the treasure

Comment [JB(]: AO1 – Major Sholto does not really need the extra treasure,

Comment [JB(]: AO1 – Major Sholto admits that avarice is 'blind and foolish',

Comment [JB(]: AO1 – Major Sholto tries to explain how it feels to be

Comment [JB(]: AO2 – The religious imagery of the 'chaplet', which is

Comment [JB(]: AO3 – Quinine is used to treat malaria and it reminds the reader

Comment [JB(]: AO1 – Even Captain Morstan is suffering from physical ills,

Comment [JB(]: AO1 – The division of the treasure causes an argument, which

Comment [JB(]: AO2 – The adjective 'heated' conveys the idea that the words

Comment [JB(]: AO2 – The word 'sprung' makes Captian Morstan appear

Comment [JB(]: AO1 – The emotional outburst shows the reader that greed and

Comment [JB(]: AO1 – Interestingly, it is literally the treasure itself that causes the

• how does Conan Doyle contrast the methods and character of
Athelney Jones with Sherlock Holmes in this extract
• how does Conan Doyle contrast the methods and character of
Athelney Jones with Sherlock Holmes in the novel as a whole.

EXTRACT

Sir Arthur Conan Doyle: The Sign of Four
Read the following extract from Chapter 6 of The Sign of
Four and then answer the question.
In this extract, Athelney Jones has just arrived to investigate
the murder of Batholomew Sholto. Thaddeus 's brother.
Holmes is expecting the arrival of the police, as he sent
Thaddeus to the police station to report the matter to them.
The extract is important for it allows the reader to compare the
work of the police, who had a poor reputation in the
nineteenth-century, with that of Holmes.

As he [Holmes] spoke, the steps which had been coming nearer
sounded loudly on the passage, and a very stout, portly man in a grey
suit strode heavily into the room. He was red-faced, burly and
plethoric, with a pair of very small twinkling eyes which looked
keenly out from between swollen and puffy pouches. He was closely
followed by an inspector in uniform, and by the still palpitating
Thaddeus Sholto.

"Here's a business!" he cried, in a muffled, husky voice. "Here's a
pretty business! But who are all these? Why, the house seems to be
as full as a rabbit-warren!"

"I think you must recollect me, Mr. Athelney Jones," said Holmes,
quietly.

"Why, of course I do!" he wheezed. "It's Mr. Sherlock Holmes, the
theorist. Remember you! I'll never forget how you lectured us all on
causes and inferences and effects in the Bishopgate jewel case. It's

---

Comment [JB(): AO2 – We can sense
the arrival of a heavy man, judging by the
'steps' which 'sounded loudly'. The sound
imagery implies that this policeman may

Comment [JB(): AO1 – The description
of Athelney Jones refers to him being
overweight and being dressed in grey.
This is contrast to the impression we get

Comment [JB(): AO2 – The use of a
triple emphasises how physically unfit
Jones is. The fact that he is 'red-faced'
implies that he has an unhealthy lifestyle

Comment [JB(): AO1 – Jones appears to
look like a pig, in this description.
AO2 – The alliteration of 'puffy pouches'
emphasises how chubby and pig-like

Comment [JB(): AO2 – The use of sound
imagery adds to the idea that Jones is
physically unfit. The word 'muffled' and
'husky' suggests that Jones finds it

Comment [JB(): AO1 – By contrast,
Holmes is 'quietly' confident that Jones
can 'recollect' him. Holmes does not feel
the need to speak loudly to assert

Comment [JB(): AO2 – Sound imagery
reveals how unfit Jones is. He clearly has a
problem breathing and speaking.

Comment [JB(): AO1 – Jones is quite
disparaging about Holmes's methods. He
believes that the super sleuth lacks
practical skills, judging by this outburst

Comment [JB(): AO1 – Jones credits
Holmes with superior knowledge and
theoretical skills, and at least remembers
some of the details of his lecture

true you set us on the right track; but you'll own now that it was more by good luck than good guidance."

"It was a piece of very simple reasoning."

"Oh, come, now, come! Never be ashamed to own up. But what is all this? Bad business! Bad business! Stern facts here,—no room for theories. How lucky that I happened to be out at Norwood over another case! I was at the station when the message arrived. What d'you think the man died of?"

"Oh, this is hardly a case for me to theorize over," said Holmes, dryly.

"No, no. Still, we can't deny that you hit the nail on the head sometimes. Dear me! Door locked, I understand. Jewels worth half a million missing. How was the window?"

"Fastened; but there are steps on the sill."

"Well, well, if it was fastened the steps could have nothing to do with the matter. That's common sense. Man might have died in a fit; but then the jewels are missing. Ha! I have a theory. These flashes come upon me at times.—Just step outside, sergeant, and you, Mr. Sholto. Your friend can remain.— What do you think of this, Holmes? Sholto was, on his own confession, with his brother last night. The brother died in a fit, on which Sholto walked off with the treasure. How's that?"

"On which the dead man very considerately got up and locked the door on the inside."

AQA-style Specimen Assessment Material 13:
Starting with this extract, write about how Conan Doyle created tension.
Write about:
• how Conan Doyle presents tension in this extract
• how Conan Doyle presents tension in the novel as a whole.

Comment [JB(]: AO1 – Jones puts Holmes's success down to 'good luck' more than skill.

Comment [JB(]: AO1 – Holmes believes his success in the Bishopgate jewel case was down to 'simple reasoning'. The clash in their respective investigative methods is clear.

Comment [JB(]: AO2 – Jones keeps repeating the same phrase, which is made more memorable by the writer's use of alliteration. It seems to be a verbal tic, but

Comment [JB(]: AO3 – Jones's belief in luck implies that he is not a very efficient police officer. At the time, there was very little confidence in the ability of the police

Comment [JB(]: AO1 – Holmes's impatience with Jones's is apparent, as his response is short and 'dryly' delivered.

Comment [JB(]: AO2 – Jones uses a hackneyed phrase to grudgingly praise Holmes. The use of the word 'sometimes' suggests understatement, as readers have

Comment [JB(]: AO1 – Jones is ready to jump to erroneous conclusions in the name of 'common sense'. This sets him apart from Holmes, who will even

Comment [JB(]: AO1 – Jones's 'theory' is laughable. He shows how incompetent he is, especially in comparison to Holmes.

Comment [JB(]: AO3 – Holmes makes Jones look ridiculous here, which ties in with the idea that police were generally thought to be unreliable and incompetent

EXTRACT

Sir Arthur Conan Doyle: The Sign of Four

Read the following extract from Chapter 10 of The Sign of Four and then answer the question.

In this extract, Holmes, Watson and Athelney Jones are in pursuit of the 'Aurora' on the Thames. This chase scene is just one example of how Conan Doyle produces tension and suspense in the novella, and this extract is important, as it is the climactic scene. If the pursuit is successful, Holmes and his associates will possibly be able to capture the criminals and the stolen treasure.

Our boilers were strained to their utmost, and the frail shell vibrated and creaked with the fierce energy which was driving us along. We had shot through the Pool, past the West India Docks, down the long Deptford Reach, and up again after rounding the Isle of Dogs. The dull blur in front of us resolved itself now clearly enough into the dainty *Aurora*. Jones turned our search-light upon her, so that we could plainly see the figures upon her deck. One man sat by the stern, with something black between his knees over which he stooped. Beside him lay a dark mass which looked like a Newfoundland dog. The boy held the tiller, while against the red glare of the furnace I could see old Smith, stripped to the waist, and shovelling coals for dear life. They may have had some doubt at first as to whether we were really pursuing them, but now as we followed every winding and turning which they took there could no longer be any question about it. At Greenwich we were about three hundred paces behind them. At Blackwall we could not have been more than two hundred and fifty. I have coursed many creatures in many countries during my checkered career, but never did sport give me such a wild thrill as this mad, flying man-hunt down the Thames. Steadily we drew in upon them, yard by yard. In the silence of the night we could hear the panting and clanking of their machinery. The man in the stern still crouched upon the deck, and his arms were moving as though he were busy, while every now and then he would look up and measure with a glance the distance which still separated us. Nearer we came and

Comment [JB(]: AO2 – The personification of the boilers being

Comment [JB(]: AO2 – The superlative 'utmost' exaggerates how strained the

Comment [JB(]: AO2 – The adjective 'frail' and the noun 'shell' add to the

Comment [JB(]: AO2 – The writer works through the senses to produce an almost

Comment [JB(]: AO3 – Like the London fog setting, elsewhere, this 'dull blur'

Comment [JB(]: AO1 – The writer uses the idea of a 'search-light' to increase the

Comment [JB(]: AO1 – The gradual revealing of exactly what is on the

Comment [JB(]: AO3 – The narrative taps into the genre of realism here, as the

Comment [JB(]: AO2 – This colloquial turn of phrase seems apt to describe 'old

Comment [JB(]: AO3 – Real place names add to the tension, as the realism created

Comment [JB(]: AO2 – The writer uses a countdown of 'three hundred paces' to

Comment [JB(]: AO2 – The writer's use of alliteration emphasises how

Comment [JB(]: AO2 – the writer uses alliteration and the metaphor of 'flying' to

Comment [JB(]: AO2 – The use of sound imagery and personification heightens the

Comment [JB(]: AO1 – Despite the search-light, not everything is apparent.

nearer. Jones yelled to them to stop. We were not more than four
boat's lengths behind them, both boats flying at a tremendous pace.

Comment [JB(]: AO2 – The writer begins to use short sentences to crank up the

Comment [JB(]: AO2 – The writer uses the metaphor of 'flying', for a second

AQA-style Specimen Assessment Material 14:
Starting with this extract, write about how Conan Doyle creates
a sense of excitement in *The Sign of Four*.
Write about:
• **how Conan Doyle presents excitement in this extract**
• **how Conan Doyle presents excitement in the novel as a whole.**

Comment [JB(]: AO1 – The writer literally tells us that both vessels are

Comment [JB(]: AO2 – The use of the metaphor 'flying' emphasises to the

EXTRACT

Comment [JB(]: AO2 – The writer uses straightforward language to re-emphasise

Sir Arthur Conan Doyle: The Sign of Four
Read the following extract from Chapter 10 of The Sign
of Four and then answer the question.
In this extract, Holmes, Watson and Athelney Jones are
pursuing the 'Aurora'. They aim to capture the criminals and
treasure on board that vessel and have just spotted her.
Holmes has noted that the 'Aurora' is 'going like the devil' and
has instructed the engineer on their boat to go at 'full speed' in
order to catch her. The extract is important as it is swiftly
nearing the climactic scene, which will involves a showdown.

Comment [JB(]: AO2 – The adverb 'gravely' suggests Jones pessimism at

Comment [JB(]: AO1 – The writer shows us through Jones's action how impossible

Comment [JB(]: AO3 – Jones is at odds with Holmes, as the former is now

Comment [JB(]: AO3 – The chase is a generic convention of detective fiction.

Comment [JB(]: AO2 – After showing Jones's doubts, the writer allows the

Now she was flying down the stream, near in to the shore, going at a
tremendous rate. Jones looked gravely at her and shook his head.

"She is very fast," he said. "I doubt if we shall catch her."

"We must catch her!" cried Holmes, between his teeth. "Heap it on,
stokers! Make her do all she can! If we burn the boat we must have
them!"

We were fairly after her now. The furnaces roared, and the powerful
engines whizzed and clanked, like a great metallic heart. Her sharp,
steep prow cut through the river-water and sent two rolling waves to
right and to left of us. With every throb of the engines we sprang and

Comment [JB(]: AO2 – The writer has Holmes's speaking in the imperative with

Comment [JB(]: AO1 – Holmes is portrayed as the most determined to

Comment [JB(]: AO1 – The narrator informs us of their progress, adding

Comment [JB(]: AO2 – A combination of personification and sound imagery adds

quivered like a living thing. One great yellow lantern in our bows
threw a long, flickering funnel of light in front of us. Right ahead a
dark blur upon the water showed where the Aurora lay, and the swirl
of white foam behind her spoke of the pace at which she was going.
We flashed past barges, steamers, merchant-vessels, in and out,
behind this one and round the other. Voices hailed us out of the
darkness, but still the Aurora thundered on, and still we followed
close upon her track.

"Pile it on, men, pile it on!" cried Holmes, looking down into the
engine-room, while the fierce glow from below beat upon his eager,
aquiline face.

AQA-style Specimen Assessment Material 15:
Starting with this extract, write about how Conan Doyle presents
the relationship between Holmes and Watson.
Write about:
• how Conan Doyle presents their relationship in this extract
• how Conan Doyle presents their relationship in the novel as a
whole.

EXTRACT

Sir Arthur Conan Doyle: The Sign of Four

Read the following extract from Chapter 1 of The Sign of
Four and then answer the question.
In this extract, Holmes and Watson are in conversation.

Holmes has been bragging about his 'several monographs',
which are pieces of writing on a specialist subject. He claims
that the differences in different types of tobacco ash are
obvious to him. The extract is important as it reminds the
reader how Watson is in awe of Holmes and how their
discussion reveals is a teacher-pupil relationship.

"You have an extraordinary genius for minutiae," I remarked.

"I appreciate their importance. Here is my monograph upon the
tracing of footsteps, with some remarks upon the uses of plaster of

---

Comment [JB(): AO2 – This simile
reminds us that pursuers are all one in
their mission to bring about justice.

Comment [JB(): AO2 – The
personification of the 'Aurora' makes the
vessel appear to be nearly impossible to
catch again.

Comment [JB(): AO2 – The metaphor
'flashed' reminds us that the craft in
pursuit is also travelling at a breakneck
speed. The list of boats passed
emphasises how these boatds are left in
their wake. Through speed comes
excitement.

Comment [JB(): AO2 – The adjective
'fierce' reminds the reader that Holmes is
a match for any criminal. His 'eager'
nature implies that he will never give up
until he has brought the criminals to

Comment [JB(): AO3 – Generically,
detective fiction is characterised by an
intelligent investigator, who is cleverer
than the other characters. Therefore, the
relationship between the two conforms

Comment [JB(): AO1 – The narrator
quickly reveals how much he admires
Holmes's skills as a detective. Holmes's
eye for details appears to be second-to-
none, according to Watson.

Comment [JB(): AO1 – Holmes clearly
feels proud of his own writing
achievement. He is lucky to have such a
receptive audience in the more passive
Watson.

Paris as a preserver of impresses. Here, too, is a curious little work upon the influence of a trade upon the form of the hand, with lithotypes of the hands of slaters, sailors, corkcutters, compositors, weavers, and diamond-polishers. That is a matter of great practical interest to the scientific detective,— especially in cases of unclaimed bodies, or in discovering the antecedents of criminals. But I weary you with my hobby."

"Not at all," I answered, earnestly. "It is of the greatest interest to me, especially since I have had the opportunity of observing your practical application of it. But you spoke just now of observation and deduction. Surely the one to some extent implies the other."

"Why, hardly," he answered, leaning back luxuriously in his armchair, and sending up thick blue wreaths from his pipe. "For example, observation shows me that you have been to the Wigmore Street Post-Office this morning, but deduction lets me know that when there you dispatched a telegram."

"Right!" said I. "Right on both points! But I confess that I don't see how you arrived at it. It was a sudden impulse upon my part, and I have mentioned it to no one."

"It is simplicity itself." he remarked, chuckling at my surprise,—

AQA-style Specimen Assessment Material 16:
Starting with this extract, write about how Conan Doyle presents the exotic.
Write about:
• how Conan Doyle presents Tonga in this extract
• how Conan Doyle presents the exotic in the novel as a whole.

EXTRACT

Sir Arthur Conan Doyle: The Sign of Four
Read the following extract from Chapter 10 of The Sign of Four and then answer the question.

Comment [JB(]: AO2 – Holmes's gloating over his achievements is

Comment [JB(]: AO3 – The study of lithotypes or imprints gives Holmes a

Comment [JB(]: AO2 – The use of a list emphasises the number of different types

Comment [JB(]: AO1 – For the first time in this extract, Holmes shows

Comment [JB(]: AO2 – The use of the superlative 'greatest' reminds the reader

Comment [JB(]: AO1 – Holmes is quite dismissive of Watson's suggestion that

Comment [JB(]: AO2 – The use of alliteration emphasises how relaxed

Comment [JB(]: AO2 – Holmes is portrayed as producing 'wreaths' of

Comment [JB(]: AO1 – Holmes spells out the clear difference between

Comment [JB(]: AO2 – The repetition of the word 'right' shows how perfect

Comment [JB(]: AO1 – Watson confesses his ignorance, which gives

Comment [JB(]: AO3 – Another generic convention found in detective fiction

Comment [JB(]: AO1 – Holmes is quite patronising towards Watson, by

Comment [JB(]: AO2 – The sound imagery of the word 'chuckling' makes it

In this extract, Holmes, Watson and Athelney Jones are closing in on the 'Aurora' after chasing the vessel up the Thames. This extract is important, as it gives the reader a glimpse of the criminals. We have just viewed the man with the wooden stump 'and now we are given a description of Tonga, who is not from England, as is therefore exotic. However, the description is far from flattering, giving us a negative view of him, while reflecting the racist attitudes and assumptions of the late Victorian era.

At the sound of his strident, angry cries there was movement in the huddled bundle upon the deck. It straightened itself into a little black man—the smallest I have ever seen—with a great, misshapen head and a shock of tangled, dishevelled hair. Holmes had already drawn his revolver, and I whipped out mine at the sight of this savage, distorted creature. He was wrapped in some sort of dark ulster or blanket, which left only his face exposed; but that face was enough to give a man a sleepless night. Never have I seen features so deeply marked with all bestiality and cruelty. His small eyes glowed and burned with a sombre light, and his thick lips were writhed back from his teeth, which grinned and chattered at us with a half animal fury.

"Fire if he raises his hand," said Holmes, quietly. We were within a boat's-length by this time, and almost within touch of our quarry. I can see the two of them now as they stood, the white man with his legs far apart, shrieking out curses, and the unhallowed dwarf with his hideous face, and his strong yellow teeth gnashing at us in the light of our lantern.

It was well that we had so clear a view of him. Even as we looked he plucked out from under his covering a short, round piece of wood, like a school-ruler, and clapped it to his lips. Our pistols rang out together. He whirled round, threw up his arms, and with a kind of choking cough fell sideways into the stream. I caught one glimpse of his venomous, menacing eyes amid the white swirl of the waters.

Comment [JB[]: AO1 – This unflattering description of the 'little black man' makes

Comment [JB[]: AO2 – The word 'shock' subtly implies that the narrator is

Comment [JB[]: AO1 – The writer conveys the idea that Tonga is wild and

Comment [JB[]: AO2 – The writer uses sibilance to emphasise the snake-like

Comment [JB[]: AO1 – The writer compares Tonga's face to the stuff of

Comment [JB[]: AO2 – The use of the hyperbolic 'never' adds to the idea that

Comment [JB[]: AO1 – The exotic Tonga is presented here as animalistic and cruel.

Comment [JB[]: AO2 – The use of semantic field of fire subtly links Tonga

Comment [JB[]: AO1 – The writer uses stereotypical racial ideas to negatively

Comment [JB[]: AO2 – Using triplets and personification, the writer conveys

Comment [JB[]: AO1 – The writer does not appear to recognise Tonga as a full

Comment [JB[]: AO3 – The language of the gothic, like 'unhallowed' and

Comment [JB[]: AO1 – The animal-like portrayal of Tonga continues as he is

Comment [JB[]: AO2 – The schoolboy simile makes Tonga's weaponry appear

Comment [JB[]: AO1 – Even when Tonga dies, there is no sympathy in the

CLOUD 9 – 'THE SIGN OF FOUR' STUDY GUIDE

AQA Specimen Assessment Material 17: 'Sherlock Holmes is a brilliant early example of a fictional detective.'
Starting with this extract, how far do you agree with this statement?
Write about:
• **how Conan Doyle presents Holmes in this extract**
• **how Conan Doyle presents Holmes in the novel as a whole.**

EXTRACT

Sir Arthur Conan Doyle: The Sign of Four
Read the following extract from Chapter 1 of The Sign of Four and then answer the question.
In this extract, Watson has just challenged Holmes to work out who is the owner of a watch. The detective has successfully deduced, using the balance of probability 'that it belonged to Watson's brother, much to the annoyance of the latter, who asks if it was guess-work'. The extract is important for it allows the reader to better understand the workings of Holmes's mind and character. Additionally, it provides us with a good explanation of deductive reasoning and how Holmes uses inference to help him solve mysteries.

"No, no: I never guess. It is a shocking habit,—destructive to the logical faculty. What seems strange to you is only so because you do not follow my train of thought or observe the small facts upon which large inferences may depend. For example, I began by stating that your brother was careless. When you observe the lower part of that watch-case you notice that it is not only dinted in two places, but it is cut and marked all over from the habit of keeping other hard objects, such as coins or keys, in the same pocket. Surely it is no great feat to assume that a man who treats a fifty-guinea watch so cavalierly must be a careless man. Neither is it a very far-fetched inference that a man who inherits one article of such value is pretty well provided for in other respects."

I nodded, to show that I followed his reasoning.

Comment [JB(]: AO2 – This emphatic statement makes Holmes appear to be extremely strange and proud of the fact that he will not lower himself to merely 'guess'. The word 'never' is normally used to exaggerate, but here we can guess that Holmes is not using hyperbole.

Comment [JB(]: AO1 – Holmes's observation of the finer details of the watch indicate that he is a man who notices literally everything.

Comment [JB(]: AO1 – Holmes's deductions are evidence of a sharp mind at work. He plays down his achievement in correctly deducing so much from so little by describing his work as 'no great feat'. However, we may feel that he is

Comment [JB(]: AO2 – Holmes's powers of deductive reasoning drive the plot, as he has to uncover all the fact to prove his theories are true. Additionally, his analysis makes him appear more like an 'automaton' (as mentioned elsewhere in

Comment [JB(]: AO1 – Holmes's deduction leads him to safely assume that Watson's brother was 'pretty well provided for'. This gives us another insight into how Holmes has become such a formidable detective. AO2 – There is

Comment [JB(]: AO2 – The word 'nodded' shows that Watson is comparatively passive compared to Holmes, who is doing all of the talking. The word 'follower', meanwhile, shows that Holmes is the undisputed leader in

"It is very customary for pawnbrokers in England, when they take a watch, to scratch the number of the ticket with a pin-point upon the inside of the case. It is more handy than a label, as there is no risk of the number being lost or transposed. There are no less than four such numbers visible to my lens on the inside of this case. Inference,— that your brother was often at low water. Secondary inference,—that he had occasional bursts of prosperity, or he could not have redeemed the pledge. Finally, I ask you to look at the inner plate, which contains the key-hole. Look at the thousands of scratches all round the hole,—marks where the key has slipped. What sober man's key could have scored those grooves? But you will never see a drunkard's watch without them. He winds it at night, and he leaves these traces of his unsteady hand. Where is the mystery in all this?"

Comment [JB(]: AO1 – Holmes's knowledge of the world is impressive, as he even knows about the practises of pawnbrokers. Given the fact that he has a housekeeper, it seems unlikely that Holmes would ever need to pawn possessions in order to borrow money.

Comment [JB(]: AO2 - The sequential markers, 'secondly' and 'finally' tell the reader that Holmes is a precise man, who logically processes information. He painstakingly chronicles how he has arrived at his conclusion for the benefit of his companion, Watson.

AQA-style Specimen Assessment Material 18:
Starting with this extract, explore how Conan Doyle creates a sense of mystery.
Write about:

• how Conan Doyle uses places to create a sense of mystery in this extract

• how Conan Doyle creates a sense of mystery in the novel as a whole.

EXTRACT

Sir Arthur Conan Doyle: The Sign of Four
Read the following extract from Chapter 3 and then answer the question.
In this extract Holmes, Watson and Mary are on their way to their first mysterious meeting. This is an important scene, in terms of plot, as the mystery may begin to unravel once the trio have arrived at their destination. Holmes mentions to Watson, the narrator,

earlier in the chapter, that their 'expedition of to-night will solve 'the 'difficulties' surrounding the case.

At first I had some idea as to the direction in which we were driving; but soon, what with our pace, the fog, and my own limited knowledge of London, I lost my bearings, and knew nothing, save that we seemed to be going a very long way. Sherlock Holmes was never at fault, however, and he muttered the names as the cab rattled through squares and in and out by tortuous by-streets.

"Rochester Row," said he. "Now Vincent Square. Now we come out on the Vauxhall Bridge Road. We are making for the Surrey side, apparently. Yes, I thought so. Now we are on the bridge. You can catch glimpses of the river."

We did indeed bet a fleeting view of a stretch of the Thames with the lamps shining upon the broad, silent water; but our cab dashed on, and was soon involved in a labyrinth of streets upon the other side.

"Wordsworth Road," said my companion. "Priory Road. Lark Hall Lane. Stockwell Place. Robert Street. Cold Harbor Lane. Our quest does not appear to take us to very fashionable regions."

We had, indeed, reached a questionable and forbidding neighborhood. Long lines of dull brick houses were only relieved by the coarse glare and tawdry brilliancy of public houses at the corner. Then came rows of two-storied villas each with a fronting of miniature garden, and then again interminable lines of new staring brick buildings,—the monster tentacles which the giant city was throwing out into the country. At last the cab drew up at the third house in a new terrace. None of the other houses were inhabited, and that at which we stopped was as dark as its neighbors, save for a single glimmer in the kitchen window.

AQA-style Specimen Assessment Material 19:
Starting with this extract, explore how Conan Doyle presents Holmes as an interesting and unusual investigator.
Write about:

Comment [JB(]: AO2 – Fog adds mystery, as it is nearly impossible for Holmes and Watson to see where they

Comment [JB(]: AO1 - Watson confesses he is unfamiliar with the settings he is passing on this mysterious

Comment [JB(]: AO1 - Holmes is portrayed as a superman, who can unravel this mystery. Using the hyperbole

Comment [JB(]: AO2 – Using sound imagery, the author makes the journey appear tense and, by default, more

Comment [JB(]: AO3 – Holmes is like a London guide, so detailed is his knowledge about the city. He is portrayed

Comment [JB(]: AO2 – The word 'labyrinth' means maze and this adds more twists and turns to the journey

Comment [JB(]: AO1 - Holmes is familiar with this mysterious route, making him appear knowledgeable and more than

Comment [JB(]: AO1 – Holmes is familiar with places on this mysterious route, which makes him appear

Comment [JB(]: AO3 - This authentic place name adds realism to the setting, while symbolically suggesting through the

Comment [JB(]: AO3 – The 'coarse' (which means rough) and 'tawdry' (which means cheap and tasteless) setting

Comment [JB(]: AO2 – The use of personification adds to the mystery, as the city appears to have as many arms as

Comment [JB(]: AO3 - The darkness of this setting makes it fall into the genre of the gothic

- how Conan Doyle presents Holmes as an interesting and unusual investigator in this extract
- how Conan Doyle presents Holmes as an interesting and unusual investigator in the novel as a whole.

EXTRACT

Sir Arthur Conan Doyle: The Sign of Four
Read the following extract from Chapter 6 of The Sign of Four and then answer the question.
In this extract, Holmes is investigating the death of Bartholomew Sholto at Pondicherry Lodge. Holmes has already deduced that one of the assassins was a man with a wooden leg and now he is discussing the child-sized prints of a naked foot 'at the scene of the crime with Watson. The extract is important for it allows the reader to gain insight into Holmes's character and to see how he operates as an expert detective.

"My dear Watson, try a little analysis yourself," said he, with a touch of impatience. "You know my methods. Apply them, and it will be instructive to compare results."

"I cannot conceive anything which will cover the facts," I answered.

"It will be clear enough to you soon," he said, in an off-hand way. "I think that there is nothing else of importance here, but I will look." He whipped out his lens and a tape measure, and hurried about the room on his knees, measuring, comparing, examining, with his long thin nose only a few inches from the planks, and his beady eyes gleaming and deep-set like those of a bird. So swift, silent, and furtive were his movements, like those of a trained blood-hound picking out a scent, that I could not but think what a terrible criminal he would have made had he turned his energy and sagacity against the law, instead of exerting them in its defense. As he hunted about, he kept muttering to himself, and finally he broke out into a loud crow of delight.

Comment [JB(]: AO1 – Holmes is instructive like a teacher to his pupil, Watson. He is an unusual investigator in

Comment [JB(]: AO3 – Holmes is presented as an expert investigator, which fits into the genre of detective

Comment [JB(]: AO1 – This equipment shows how well prepared Holmes is. It is interesting for the reader, who might

Comment [JB(]: AO2 – It is almost as if Holmes worships his job of solving crimes, metaphorically at least

Comment [JB(]: AO2 – Ascending tricolon is used here to show the details of the process that Holmes goes through

Comment [JB(]: AO1 – This shows how keen Holmes is to solves the crime. He is completely immersed in that activity and

Comment [JB(]: AO2 – Bird imagery makes Holmes appear to be intelligent and focused, implying that almost like a

Comment [JB(]: AO2 - This triplet emphasises how formidable Holmes's detective skills are

Comment [JB(]: AO2 – Blood-hound imagery makes Holmes appear to be a sleuth who will never give up his pursuit

Comment [JB(]: AO1 – The narrator makes it clear that he feels the world is lucky that Holmes has chosen to be on

Comment [JB(]: AO1 – This portrays Holmes as eccentric and enthusiastic. He is completely absorbed in his task

Comment [JB(]: AO2 – Sound imagery links Holmes to birds again. Crows are birds that are known for their intelligence

"We are certainly in luck," said he. "We ought to have very little trouble now. Number One has had the misfortune to tread in the creosote. You can see the outline of the edge of his small foot here at the side of this evil-smelling mess. The carboy has been cracked, You see, and the stuff has leaked out."

AQA-style Specimen Assessment Material 20:
Starting with this extract, write about how Conan Doyle presents Mary Morstan.
Write about:
• how Conan Doyle presents Mary Morstan in this extract
• how Conan Doyle presents Mary Morstan in the novel as a whole.

EXTRACT

Sir Arthur Conan Doyle: The Sign of Four
Read the following extract from Chapter 2 of The Sign of Four and then answer the question.
In this extract, Holmes and Watson are awaiting the arrival of Miss Mary Morstan. They have already been informed of her name by their landlady, Mrs Hudson, who describes her as 'a young lady'. The extract is important for it allows the reader to get a chance to form an opinion of this female character, whose mystery will drive the plot forward.

Miss Morstan entered the room with a firm step and an outward composure of manner. She was a blonde young lady, small, dainty, well gloved, and dressed in the most perfect taste. There was, however, a plainness and simplicity about her costume which bore with it a suggestion of limited means. The dress was a sombre grayish beige, untrimmed and unbraided, and she wore a small turban of the same dull hue, relieved only by a suspicion of white feather in the side. Her face had neither regularity of feature nor beauty of complexion, but her expression was sweet and amiable, and her large blue eyes were singularly spiritual and sympathetic. In an experience of women which

Comment [JB(]: AO1 – Although the reader can sense that Holmes makes his own luck, he does enjoy the moments

Comment [JB(]: AO3 – There is a hint of the gothic in this mention of the word 'evil', which ostensibly is olfactory

Comment [JB(]: AO3 – Holmes's knowledge of the world is unparalleled. He understands the contemporary world

Comment [JB(]: AO1 – Mary's strength of purpose is apparent from the beginning, as she enters the room

Comment [JB(]: AO2 – A succession of adjectives detail Mary's feminine features, making her appear attractive

Comment [JB(]: AO2 – A superlative is used here and indicates exaggeration on the part of the narrator, Watson. It could

Comment [JB(]: AO1 – These adjectives indicate that Mary is modest and restrains herself when it comes to choosing her

Comment [JB(]: AO1 – The narrator has quickly decided that Mary may be suffering from some financial problems

Comment [JB(]: AO2 – Negative adjectives add to the idea that something is lacking in Mary's life; money

Comment [JB(]: AO3 – The 'turban' is exotic head wear that links Mary to the British Empire and, in particular, India

Comment [JB(]: AO1 – The writer appears to be setting Mary up as a love interest for Watson, judging by these

Comment [JB(]: AO2 – The writer uses the sibilance of the words 'spiritual and sympathetic' and soothing 's' sounds to

extends over many nations and three separate continents, I have never looked upon a face which gave a clearer promise of a refined and sensitive nature. I could not but observe that as she took the seat which Sherlock Holmes placed for her, her lip trembled, her hand quivered, and she showed every sign of intense inward agitation.

"I have come to you, Mr. Holmes," she said, "because you once enabled my employer, Mrs. Cecil Forrester, to unravel a little domestic complication. She was much impressed by your kindness and
skill."

"Mrs. Cecil Forrester," he repeated thoughtfully. "I believe that I was of some slight service to her. The case, however, as I remember it, was a very simple one."

"She did not think so. But at least you cannot say the same of mine. I can hardly imagine anything more strange, more utterly inexplicable, than the situation in which I find myself."

Comment [JB(]: AO3 – Mary is being portrayed as the ideal Victorian woman, as she seems cultured and delicate, which would have been attributes that would have been very much appreciated at the time. It was uncommon for women to try to gain certain skills, which were referred to as 'accomplishments' (like playing the piano), which defined them as women.

Comment [JB(]: AO2 – The writer uses a triplet to emphasise how feminine Mary is.
AO3 - She completely conforms to the Victorian female stereotype of being quite frail and never far from fainting.
AO1 – The situation is causing her a lot of heartache, judging by the 'inward agitation'.

Comment [JB(]: AO3 – She is portrayed as a damsel in distress, which allows the male characters, in this case Watson, to behave with chivalry.

Comment [JB(]: AO3 – Victorian women are usually associated with the home.

Comment [JB(]: AO2 – Her need for help is a catalyst for the narrative.

CLOUD 9 – 'THE SIGN OF FOUR' STUDY GUIDE

Essay writing tips

<u>Use a variety of connectives</u>

Have a look of this list of connectives. Which of these would you choose to use?

'ADDING' DISCOURSE MARKERS

- AND

- ALSO

- AS WELL AS

- MOREOVER

- TOO

- FURTHERMORE

- ADDITIONALLY

I hope you chose 'additionally', 'furthermore' and 'moreover'. Don't be afraid to use the lesser discourse markers, as they are also useful. Just avoid using those ones over and over again. I've seen essays from Key Stage 4 students that use the same discourse marker for the opening sentence of each paragraph! Needless to say, those essays didn't get great marks!

Okay, here are some more connectives for you to look at. Select the best ones.

'SEQUENCING' DISCOURSE MARKERS

- NEXT

- FIRSTLY

- SECONDLY

- THIRDLY

- FINALLY

- MEANWHILE

- AFTER

- THEN

- SUBSEQUENTLY

This time, I hope you chose 'subsequently' and 'meanwhile'.

Here are some more connectives for you to 'grade'!

'ILLUSTRATING / EXEMPLIFYING' DISCOURSE MARKERS

- FOR EXAMPLE

- SUCH AS

- FOR INSTANCE

- IN THE CASE OF

- AS REVEALED BY

- ILLUSTRATED BY

CLOUD 9 – 'THE SIGN OF FOUR' STUDY GUIDE

I'd probably go for 'illustrated by' or even 'as exemplified by' (which is not in the list!). Please feel free to add your own examples to the lists. Strong connectives impress examiners. Don't forget it! That's why I want you to look at some more.

'CAUSE & EFFECT' DISCOURSE MARKERS

- BECAUSE

- SO

- THEREFORE

- THUS

- CONSEQUENTLY

- HENCE

I'm going for 'consequently' this time. How about you? What about the next batch?

'COMPARING' DISCOURSE MARKERS

- SIMILARLY

- LIKEWISE

- AS WITH

- LIKE

- EQUALLY

- IN THE SAME WAY

I'd choose 'similarly' this time. Still some more to go.

'QUALIFYING' DISCOURSE MARKERS

- BUT
- HOWEVER
- WHILE
- ALTHOUGH
- UNLESS
- EXCEPT
- APART FROM
- AS LONG AS

It's 'however' for me!

'CONTRASTING' DISCOURSE MARKERS

- WHEREAS
- INSTEAD OF
- ALTERNATIVELY
- OTHERWISE
- UNLIKE
- ON THE OTHER HAND
- CONVERSELY

I'll take 'conversely' or 'alternatively' this time.

'EMPHASISING' DISCOURSE MARKERS

- ABOVE ALL

- IN PARTICULAR

- ESPECIALLY

- SIGNIFICANTLY

- INDEED

- NOTABLY

You can breathe a sigh of relief now! It's over! No more connectives. However, now I want to put our new found skills to use in our essays.

Useful information/Glossary

Allegory: extended metaphor, like the grim reaper representing death, e.g. Scrooge symbolizing capitalism.

Alliteration: same consonant sound repeating, e.g. 'She sells sea shells'.

Allusion: reference to another text/person/place/event.

Ascending tricolon: sentence with three parts, each increasing in power, e.g. 'ringing, drumming, shouting'.

Aside: character speaking so some characters cannot hear what is being said. Sometimes, an aside is directly to the audience. It's a dramatic technique which reveals the character's inner thoughts and feelings.

Assonance: same vowel sounds repeating, e.g. 'Oh no, won't Joe go?'

Bathos: abrupt change from sublime to ridiculous for humorous effect.

Blank verse: lines of unrhymed iambic pentameter.

Compressed time: when the narrative is fast-forwarding through the action.

Descending tricolon: sentence with three parts, each decreasing in power, e.g. 'shouting, talking, whispering'.

Denouement: tying up loose ends, the resolution.

Diction: choice of words or vocabulary.

Didactic: used to describe literature designed to inform, instruct or pass on a moral message.

Dilated time: opposite compressed time, here the narrative is in slow motion.

CLOUD 9 – 'THE SIGN OF FOUR' STUDY GUIDE

Direct address: second person narrative, predominantly using the personal pronoun 'you'.

Dramatic action verb: manifests itself in physical action, e.g. I punched him in the face.

Dramatic irony: audience knows something that the character is unaware of.

Ellipsis: leaving out part of the story and allowing the reader to fill in the narrative gap.

End-stopped lines: poetic lines that end with punctuation.

Epistolary: letter or correspondence-driven narrative.

Flashback/Analepsis: going back in time to the past, interrupting the chronological sequence.

Flashforward/Prolepsis: going forward in time to the future, interrupting the chronological sequence.

Foreshadowing/Adumbrating: suggestion of plot developments that will occur later in the narrative.

Gothic: another strand of Romanticism, typically with a wild setting, a sensitive heroine, an older man with a 'piercing gaze', discontinuous structure, doppelgangers, guilt and the 'unspeakable' (according to Eve Kosofsky Sedgwick).

Hamartia: character flaw, leading to that character's downfall.

Hyperbole: exaggeration for effect.

Iambic pentameter: a line of ten syllables beginning with a lighter stress alternating with a heavier stress in its perfect form, which sounds like a heartbeat. The stress falls on the even syllables, numbers: 2, 4, 6, 8 and 10, e.g. 'When now I think you can behold such sights'.

Intertextuality: links to other literary texts.

Irony: amusing or cruel reversal of expected outcome or words meaning the opposite to their literal meaning.

Metafiction/Romantic irony: self-conscious exposure of the devices used to create 'the truth' within a work of fiction.

Motif: recurring image use of language or idea that connects the narrative together and creates a theme or mood, e.g. 'green light' in *The Great Gatsby*.

Oxymoron: contradictory terms combined, e.g. deafening silence.

Pastiche: imitation of another's work.

Pathetic fallacy: a form of personification whereby inanimate objects show human attributes, e.g. 'the sea smiled benignly'. The originator of the term, John Ruskin in 1856, used 'the cruel, crawling foam', from Kingsley's *The Sands of Dee*, as an example to clarify what he meant by the 'morbid' nature of pathetic fallacy.

Personification: concrete or abstract object made human, often simply achieved by using a capital letter or a personal pronoun, e.g. 'Nature', or describing a ship as 'she'.

Pun/Double entendre: a word with a double meaning, usually employed in witty wordplay but not always.

Retrospective: account of events after they have occurred.

Romanticism: genre celebrating the power of imagination, spriritualism and nature.

Semantic/lexical field: related words about a single concept, e.g. king, queen and prince are all concerned with royalty.

Soliloquy: character thinks aloud, but is not heard by other characters (unlike in a monologue) giving the audience access to inner thoughts and feelings.

Style: choice of language, form and structure, and effects produced.

Synecdoche: one part of something referring to the whole, e.g. Carker's teeth represent him in *Dombey and Son*.

Syntax: the way words and sentences are placed together.

Tetracolon climax: sentence with four parts, culminating with the last part, e.g. 'I have nothing to offer but blood, toil, tears, and sweat ' (Winston Churchill).

ABOUT THE AUTHOR

Joe Broadfoot is a secondary school teacher of English and a soccer journalist, who also writes fiction and literary criticism. His former experiences as a DJ took him to far-flung places such as Tokyo, Kobe, Beijing, Hong Kong, Jakarta, Cairo, Dubai, Cannes, Oslo, Bergen and Bodo. He is now PGCE and CELTA-qualified with QTS, a first-class honours degree in Literature and an MA in Victorian Studies (majoring in Charles Dickens). Drama is close to his heart as he acted in 'Macbeth' and 'A Midsummer Night's Dream' at the Royal Northern College of Music in Manchester. More recently, he has been teaching 'A' Level and GCSE English Literature and IGCSE and GCSE English Language to students at secondary schools in Buckinghamshire, Kent and in south and west London.

21119766R00047

Printed in Poland
by Amazon Fulfillment
Poland Sp. z o.o., Wrocław